The A-Z of Curious

Lincolnshire

Stephen Wade

The History Press

First published 2011

The History Press
The Mill, Brimscombe Port
Stroud, Gloucestershire, GL5 2QG
www.thehistorypress.co.uk

British Library Cataloguing in Publication Data.
A catalogue record for this book is available from the British Library.

ISBN 978 0 7524 6027 7

Typesetting and origination by The History Press
Printed and bound in Great Britain by
Marston Book Services Ltd, Oxfordshire

Contents

Acknowledgements

THANKS GO to several people who helped with the gathering of these tales. I have to thank previous folklore writers, and all Lincolnshire researchers in this respect owe a debt to Ethel Rudkin, whose collection *Lincolnshire Folklore* is a treasure chest of tales. Help came also from Vicki Schofield, Brian Longbone and Kate Walker. Finally, I would also like to thank the photographers whose outstanding work, made available through Wikimedia Commons, I have drawn upon throughout this book: John Illingworth; Richard Croft; Jorn Brauns; David Wright; Tony Atkin; Robin Jones; Editor5807; Matthew Smith; Peter Church; and Brian Robert Marshall.

Introduction
Fact and Folklore

'Through folklore it is possible to obtain a deeper knowledge of the past than through documents.'

M.A. Murray

CURIOUS TALES are always intriguing; they fall somewhere between history and hearsay, sometimes in that muddle where folklore and tradition meet. The most common phrase associated with the 'curious' tale is 'it is said that …' In the standard paranormal story that phrase is constantly repeated. It suggests that there is some accredited acknowledgement that a tale may be valid, at least in a certain locality. More generally, even the most thorough and logical-minded social historian would have to admit that, all too often, history and folklore coalesce. We can see that most clearly in such complex and varied narratives as those of Dick Turpin (a story with a strong Lincolnshire connection) and in Robin Hood. There is supposed established history and then there is oral tradition and local lore. However, even the history in the books is not solid. In 2009, a scholar proved conclusively that the Battle of Bosworth (1485) did not take place where the heritage-centred battlefield experience said it was.

'Curious' also implies that the storyteller can be as much in the dark about the supposed truth of a tale as the listener or reader. One old rhyme expresses this characteristic:

Ladies and jelly-beans, hobos and tramps,
Cross-eyed mosquitoes and bow-legged ants.
I come before you to stand behind ye
To tell you something I know nothing about

Dick Turpin in his cave – but was this story fact or fiction?

Even the place names of the county are often extremely curious. Few areas can boast such names as Mavis Enderby or Boothby Graffoe. The scholarly *Oxford Dictionary of British Place-Names* states that the former is explained accordingly: 'Enderby – farmstead or village of a man called Eindrithi', and adds, 'The affix *mavis* is manorial from the Malebisse family.' In spite of that, there is something inbuilt within us that wants to retain the curiousness of these oddities and speculate on stories about 'Mavis' and who she was. Such is the clash of history and folklore.

In Lincolnshire, the county has long had its enthusiasts for those stories where history and tradition meet; Ethel Rudkin was no doubt the doyenne of Lincolnshire folklore, and the Society for Lincolnshire History and Archaeology has done a magnificent job in promoting this area of history, along with every other conceivable branch of the subject. I am indebted to their publications for some of my sources. Selection has not been easy; in the last decade or so there has been a flowering of small, local publication, much of it dealing with memoirs and oral history. That has been useful. Fortunately, although I am a Yorkshireman, I have lived in Lincolnshire for thirty-six years and most of the places I write about in the following pages I have seen, walked through or at least studied from photographs and press reports.

My aim here has been to select a mix of established tales along with little-known ones. Over the centuries there have been Lincolnshire tales in well-established folklore, but there are also countless stories of eccentric characters, fascinating places, inscrutable objects and no end of topographical curios. Some tales, of course, have had to be left out, but I have purposely recalled several stories relating to my special interests of crime and paranormal. It has to be commented that, strangely, the county has not received the attention given to other, much smaller counties in this respect. I suspect that has a lot to do with the inherent reticence here; after all, our greatest poet, Alfred Tennyson from Somersby, has very little presence here in the tourist industry, compared with, say, Thomas Hardy of Wessex or the Brontës of Yorkshire.

Yet Lincolnshire has endless adventures, dramas and sensations in its social history, from the seafaring men of the Humber, Grimsby and Boston to the battles and prisons of Lincoln, and from the grandeur of Burghley House and Tattershall to the industrial grit of Scunthorpe's steel industry and Gainsborough's waterways. The county also has several giants of English history in its honours list, of course; most notably Isaac Newton, John Wesley and John Harrison. But there is still much to learn about the 'yellowbelly county', and its fascinating history offers stories that should be shared and relished. I hope that *An A – Z of Curious Lincolnshire* will help in this crusade to generate more Lincolnshire knowledge and a richer sense of place. Most of my stories involve people, and a poet once memorably said that writing about people, rather than ideas and abstracts, is sure to make the ideas more accessible and clear. My stories often exist on the borderland between local history and world history; we all have a secret interior life, and we all have individual dreams and aspirations; sometimes these are contiguous to the great narratives of historical process and change. 'Curious' tales often shine a torch onto these previously shady areas of history.

Writing almost a century ago, W.F. Rawnsley commented that the word 'strange' was 'perhaps the commonest adverbial epithet in general use in Lincolnshire.' The following stories will confirm that the adjective still applies, and the mysteries remain, in spite of the relentless forces of modernity.

The east view of Tattershall Castle, Lincolnshire, at the end of the eighteenth century.

Lincoln in the early
nineteenth century.

I have mixed stories from all ages and of all kinds, though there is a predominance of tales involving the law and the paranormal. But running through all the stories is a celebration of the absurd, the bizarre and the unexpected. History is so often best understood through its local tales and affairs with 'a local habitation and a name', as Shakespeare said. For some of these, I have had to dig into the archives, whereas others are well-known within the county, although visitors may not be familiar with the traditions. Even the famous Lincoln Imp is perhaps better known as a pub name than a legend to people visiting for the first time – there are pubs of that name in Lincoln and in Scunthorpe, for instance. Folk tales, legends and mysteries will always run together into the chronicles of written history, and we will always want their strange explanations, just as much as we want the supposed 'truth' of the past.

Finally, as I have used an A–Z format, I had to be suitably inventive to find entries for all letters. 'Z' was particularly challenging, so I have the strange journey of the giraffes from Barnsley to Cleethorpes to thank for the fact that I was able to complete my A–Z without stretching credulity too far. Above all, I wanted to fulfil Lewis Carroll's twisted grammar in *Alice in Wonderland*: 'Curiouser and curiouser.'

Stephen Wade, 2011

A

⁕ ALKBOROUGH AND THE KNIGHTS ⁕

Tales of the knights who took part in the murder of Thomas Beckett in 1170 are well-known in Lincolnshire. One tradition has William de Tracey, one of the killers, living in Twigmoor. But what we do know is that he, together with Richard de Brito and Hugh de Morville, two more of the assassins, built the church at Alkborough on the Humber estuary, and until 1690 there was an inscribed stone in the chancel of the church to that effect.

In that church, St John the Baptist's, the stone was reported by Abraham de la Prynne, writing in 1697. It had a Latin inscription, which translated as:

> Richard Brito as well as Hugh Morville and William Tracey, built with
> Stones this lofty temple, a worthy glory to God.

Tradition has it that the knights took refuge in Alkborough after committing the murder.

De la Prynne had another, equally intriguing, Alkborough tale. He wrote that Kell Well, a spring below the top of the cliff at Walcot, had petrifying properties. Apparently, there were surrounding it 'a great many pretty stones, being a kind of *astroites* or star stones ... the county people call them kestles and postles.' These were kinds of fossils, in fact.

Prynne clearly loved a good myth and enjoyed speculating on the relevance of his surroundings. It is certainly a spring, but there is no record of the waters ever petrifying anything.

The martyrdom of Becket, after a painting in the Chapel of the Holy Cross, Stratford.

Alkborough's best known landmark is Julian's Bower, a turf maze over 40ft wide, supposedly created by monks in the fifteenth century, but it may be from Roman times. In the 1920s, writer W.J. Rawnsley said that the maze was thought to be similar to a game called the 'Troy', which is described in Virgil's epic poem *The Aeneid*. He refers to a similar turf-cut maze by the Solway called 'The Walls of Troy'. Regarding the mazes he added, 'Doubtless they served as innocent recreation for the monks.'

⚜ ANGEL VISITS GAINSBOROUGH ⚜

Today we have a fascination with angels. There are books in print about dealing with one's personal angel and about how we should cultivate relationships with guardian angels. The sources of the stories may be doubtful, and in such accounts we tend to check out the credentials of the teller. This story involved a witness and storyteller who was a clergyman, and he was not the alone when he saw what he saw.

Sorting through the historical papers in a small publication from some decades ago, the strangest paranormal story surely ever told of

Gainsborough was related, and it was a story that was verified by two ministers of the church and three honest, respectable gentlemen of the town. It all happened on 4 April 1819. Events began when the church bells tolled most sweetly. This would have been most welcome – except for the fact that John Coulston, who was clerk, and the sexton, had the keys. There was a locked church, with nobody inside, but still a wonderful peal of bells.

Mr King, the clergyman, was due to preach that day, and the two men went to fetch him. As the three men entered the church, King said a prayer. He was seemingly expecting something inexplicable (rather than a mere prankster): 'Our Heavenly father, we surrender ourselves at Thy call', he said as they went in, fearfully, to see what was happening.

They reached the belfry and looked around. After a few seconds they saw a child, 'clothed in white, with a crown of gold on his head and who by means alone of the breath of his mouth, put the bells in motion, and made them ring harmoniously …' King asked the child who he was, and in response the child claimed to be the messenger of the Lord: 'I am come to exhort all men to repentance.'

A vision of Heaven: an angel appearing to Joachim, by Dürer. (Library of Congress, Prints & Photographs Division, LC-USZ62-99459)

The angel's words seem close to that of a street-corner preacher, as he talked about preparing them 'for the terrible day of the last judgement when the world shall be destroyed by fire.' It was a hell and brimstone sermon from the child. He said that the Lord would 'torment the Christian nations in his anger.' King spoke again to the angel: 'How knowest thou these things?'

'My Heavenly master does not deliver them to his servants, but he has sent me ...'

The most stunning experience was to follow. The angel led the men to the interior and told them to lift a stone. None of the men could lift it, but the angel-child did so effortlessly, and he took a scroll of paper from underneath. He read the words, 'England ... renounce thy wickedness and hasten to repentance.'

The angel then disappeared – apparently to the sound of melodious music, according to the startled men. The witnesses to this bizarre experience wrote their names and dated the vision: on 4 April 1819 this strange incident unfolded – 'Mr King and Mr Horn, Ministers; Mr Chambers, John Coulston and John Boon, gentlemen.'

⚜ BARONS AND BAILIFFS ⚜

In 1255 King Henry III was taking on the powerful barons of the kingdom, trying to wrest back some authority. It became a matter of economic influence and, as always in these things, the other poor folk in the kingdom suffered as the repercussions affected the lower classes of society. The great landmark of the Magna Carta of 1215 was within living memory for many at the time. The King issued patents to the local power-base – and along came the choking monopolies of trade.

In Grimsby, the fishermen reached the point at which they had to trade abroad rather than in their home town. One earlier writer noted that the result of this was that, 'The town of Grimsby became a theatre of strife and the lower class of its inhabitants accused the opulent burgesses of a lawless and violent usurpation of their liberties.' The central forces of law had to act and, inevitably, mayhem followed. Gilbert de Preston arrived with the brief of making a report on what was going on.

The aristocrats and wealthy merchants were holding ships at sea or in harbour and then buying the cargoes very cheaply; they could then resell at an immense profit and the poor traders were being squeezed out. Of course, this was illegal – it was technically 'forestalling' – but this time, unusually in criminal history, the rich were acting like pirates. Gilbert could understand this, but could do nothing to stop a local civil war situation ensuing. Some of the stronger and less malleable characters took on William de Waltham and his pals. First, one Simon de Watchet grabbed Holm manor and blocked the roads. He strung an iron chain across the Weelby road and charged a toll. With this, sides were taken and allies asked to help. The bailiff of the Earl of Lincoln told his servants to seize a horse and cart belonging to a town burgess. Amazingly, he managed to imprison this man with his family in a gaol at Waltham. They could only be freed when the sum of ten marks was paid to Roger. He made a habit of this and his servants were becoming no more than a criminal gang. A man called Alan de Kyrketon was brave enough to take them on – and he paid the price, as he was severely beaten up and left, mortally wounded.

The fight accelerated then, as Walter de la Lindes of Little Cotes took hold of the port of Friskney. When people stood up to him, they were locked up at Laceby. His men stole goods, refused to pay taxes and generally dominated fiercely in a place where there should have been free trade and open commerce to all townspeople in a chartered borough. This was anarchy, something that the whole state had known before in several reigns, and notably in the years of Stephen and Matilda a century earlier. Even the religious principals were subject to these aggressive constraints on land and roads. The Abbot of Wellow blocked a road and the Knights Templar, who were powerful feudal magnates in the town, dammed a stream and cut off fresh water for ordinary folk.

Crown property had been taken by force and by private individuals; something had to be done before a new corporation charter could be given. A bailiffs' court was instituted to try and set things right; any further escalation of these open quarrels and abuses would have led to violence and murder. In 1259 an investigation led to a provision that merchants had to sell their goods within markets established by tradition and common goodwill. It was meant to protect the civil liberties of the weaker or less wealthy town burgesses. Through all these terrible events there were private injuries and open quarrels, as one writer has put it. That is a way of explaining the kind of resentment and aggression that leads to the worst kind of civil unrest and riot. In the centuries before an established police force, the general pattern of legal and moral obligations could easily slip into the anarchy of clannish vendetta and a 'might is right' frame of mind. One effect of all this was that soon after this turbulent period the Templars in the town were dissolved. It is a mark of the power of the burgesses and the landed aristocrats like de Lindes that this could be achieved.

The Magna Carta and its associations.

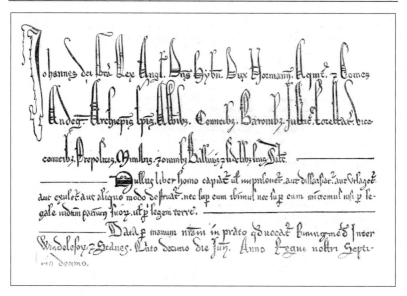

A section of the Magna Carta.

In the end, these troubles had to stop before they moved into much broader arenas of commercial allegiances and drew in factions from afar. It was a close-run affair and many must have feared the worst.

⚜ BELVOIR WITCH CASE ⚜

In 1619, witch fever gripped Leicestershire: nine women there had been hanged. By the time gossip appeared about the Flower family in the Vale of Belvoir a short while later, the moral panic was accelerating. By the early months of 1619, two sisters, Margaret and Phillipa Flower, were being examined by magistrates and in March they sat before a Grand Jury. Witchcraft was blamed by many for the troubles in the state and in the very heart of the monarchy. James I had written on the subject, and of course there had been high-profile witch trials in many parts of the land. But now, in the domains of the Earl of Rutland, these nine women had been accused of sorcery. They were destined to hang at Lincoln.

What had the Flower sisters done? A pamphlet printed in London later in the year 1619 states that they were specially arraigned before the judges 'for confessing themselves actors in the destruction of Henry, Lord

James I of England (and VI of Scotland), said to have personally attended the questioning of women accused of witchcraft.

Rosse, with their damnable practices against others of the children of the Right Honourable Francis, Earle of Rutland.' The rest is a mixture of gossip, sensation and distortion, such as stating that their mother, Joan, was 'a monstrous malicious woman'. They were supposed to have learned 'the manner of incantations, spells and charms', and then the son of the Rosse family, Henry, 'sickened very strangely and after a while died ...'

Evidence was given by two women, Ann Baker and Joan Willimot, but there was no torture, as popular cultural narratives about witches might have us believe. The most informed writer on the subject, Michael Honeybone, is sure that the two sisters' own statements were what really condemned them. Although there is no record of what actually was said and done at the Lincoln trial, it seems right to assume that, as they had confessed under examination, and then accused each other, the justices were convinced that there had been attempts to communicate with the Devil. The sisters were hanged in Lincoln Castle.

Contrary to popular belief, witches were not burned at the stake at this time. It is alarming to realise that when a woman had murdered her husband (a petit treason), she was punishable by burning, not hanging – as in the case of Eleanor Elsom in 1722. Witchcraft, on the other hand, was a felony and was on the long list of offences punishable by hanging. The first Witchcraft Act was in 1542 and was soon repealed; then in two Acts established in 1563 and 1604, harsher measures were put into force. But for most of the Middle Ages, because so many offences could involve image-making and references to Satan, the definition of witchcraft had to be specific.

Across the border in Scotland, and on the continent, the Flower sisters would have burned. In Lincoln, they walked to the Cobb Hall tower to hang.

Witch fever! An illustration of the famous Salem witch trials. (Library of Congress, Prints & Photographs Division, LC-USZ62-475)

⁘ BLACK DOG TALES ⁘

Stories of ghostly dogs are legion across Britain. They all have different local names, from the black shuck of East Anglia to the Gytrash of Yorkshire. In Lincolnshire, most experiences of seeing and hearing these spectral dogs have been in clusters around Brigg, on the Trent, and in the Fens. There is a particular area where there have been a number of sightings – in Laughton Forest north of Gainsborough. The origins of the black shuck lie somewhere between medieval folklore and the testimony of witnesses who have spoken to historians and paranormal investigators. It has never been clear exactly what the black shuck is, as interpretations vary.

It is best to begin with an actual story. An ex-police officer, a man very fond of his Alsatians, went for a morning walk with his dogs in Laughton Forest. He reported that after playing for a while, the two dogs froze and stared towards a specific spot in the undergrowth. They would not go any nearer to the vegetation and began to growl. This was totally out of character, the man revealed in an interview. He went closer, and saw a pair of eyes in the undergrowth – and then something moved. He saw the dimensions and said that the animal was the size of a horse, not a dog. He ran from the spot, back into his car, where the dogs were already sitting, shaking with terror. He drove off speedily. 'It couldn't have been a puma or any kind of big cat,' he said, 'I saw the outline of its back. It was like a racehorse.'

As far back as 1577, in Bungay, Suffolk, there have been accounts of these Black Dogs entering churches and homes, and creating havoc. One researcher, Theo Brown, has written that there were thirty-nine incidents involving a black shuck between 1829 and 1958 – incidents that were hard to explain away by rational means. Some of the earlier accounts talk of a shape-shifting dog of enormous size. But there are two notable experiences in fairly recent times, which show that Lincolnshire seems to be a focus for these apparitions.

The first was recalled by a tramp who had been walking from Caenby to Stow. He said that as he walked at dusk, not far from Glentham, where there is a sharp dip as the escarpment falls towards the North Nottingham plain, he became aware of a 'companion'. He sensed from the corner of his eye that it was taller than he, and that there was a smell, as if some cloth or skin was burning. Finally he dared to look sideways. He expected to see a fellow hobo, but instead found a Black Dog, 'the size of a small horse, its eyes yellow and its breath stinky like candle smell, like tallow …' He didn't know whether to sit, try to hide or run for it. But as he thought about his options, it walked sideways away from him and vanished.

Then there was the soldier in the 1940s, home from the war and unable to find a lift to Brigg. He reported seeing a huge dog in the afternoon, during summer, by Twigmoor woods. He swore that he had no whisky on him and had not taken a drop, but described the apparition as 'somehow not threatening … like some freak of nature but not interested in me'. It walked off in another direction as he was cowering in the bushes, praying.

Writing in 1951, Alasdair MacGregor gathered some Black Dog stories, some from the famous Lincolnshire folklorist, Ethel Rudkin of Willoughton. One story was from Kesteven, in Haconby. A brother and sister, walking near their home in the 1930s, used to take a shortcut in the dark, and walk through Bourne Wood. On more than one occasion the Black Dog would come to walk by them. It walked as far as a hand-gate.

Even more documented is the presence of the Black Dog in the Isle of Axholme, notably around Gunthorpe. Ethel Rudkin had a memory from a man there; he said he had seen the Black Dog in Intake Lane, and that his friend Sammy Prettle had once tried to shoot it. The man said, 'Sammy once shot at it by a big willow tree and his gun-barrel busted, and he came home white as a sheet.'

Arguably the most haunted spot for Black Dog appearances in the county is Belle Hole near Kirton in Lindsey. At a meeting of local historians in 1936 the Black Dog was discussed, and a local school mistress revealed, 'I often see him while cycling back to Manton alone, after a lecture or a whist-drive at Kirton.'

At Belle Hole during the same period, locals claimed that they knew where the Black Dog lived. MacGregor wrote:

That the country people believe implicitly in the existence of the Black Dog at Belle Hole is shown by the readiness with which they identify, in the bank of a stream there, the hole in which they say he lives ... In 1935 a farmer's wife at Belle Hole actually saw the Black Dog enter the farmhouse kitchen, where she happened to be at the time. She watched him as he walked round it and then left as he had entered. She remained perfectly still throughout the duration of his visit.

Experiences with the Black Dog around Grayingham, Kirton and Willoughton seem to have been frequent occurrences in the early and middle years of the last century. One woman in Grayingham said that she met the dog once and tried to strike it with her umbrella. She said that 'the umbrella went clean thruff 'im.'

What is to be made of these sightings? Maybe they lie somewhere between hallucinatory visions and distortions of something else. Most rational arguments say that the dogs are more likely to be pumas, but seen from unusual angles. Whatever perspective we take, the truth is that the sightings go on, and many have features in common. Lincolnshire appears to be one of the places they move about in, occasionally revealing themselves to people.

⸎ BULLS ON ST BRICE'S DAY ⸎

England's social history and folklore is brimming with tales of animal abuse and misuse. It is one of the less pleasant aspects of our past, as in dog-fights and cock-fights. We also used to bait bears, and that is something to be ashamed of. But less well-known is the occurrence of bull-running, more common in countries such as Spain.

In Lincolnshire, this recreation happened on St Brice's Day. The date of that feast was 13 November. St Brice himself was not exactly a good role model for a local saint: he was a proud and arrogant man, who eventually had to go and ask for pardon from St Martin, who had raised him. But as Bishop of Tours, Brice neglected his duties and was less than desirable as a leader of men. He went away into exile, did some serious thinking, and went back home a changed man – hence his eventual sainthood.

The game is supposed to have begun when two butchers noticed a pair of bulls fighting in a field. The men tried to break up the fight, but sadly, they let loose the wild bulls into the road. When the Earl Warren saw them on the loose, he set off in pursuit, and he enjoyed it so much that he thought it should be something shared by all. He allotted a special field for the game to be held, and such places became known as 'Bull Meadows' – as in Stamford, for instance.

Wealthy folk left money to finance the tradition and so it carried on. Even a mayor and churchwardens left money to pay for the tradition. It was certainly exciting, as this account shows:

> During the seventeenth century, the bull was placed overnight in a stable belonging to the alderman, in readiness for the sport. On the morning of St Brice's Day proclamation was made by the two bellmen to the following effect: each person was to shut up his shop door or gate, and none were to do any violence to strangers and a guard was appointed for the passing of travellers without hurt.

With the English sense of fair play, rules were made about what could be used against the animals in the pursuit. There was no iron allowed on the clubs carried by the men, for instance.

The bull was set out into the field and all other gates locked. The chase involved everyone in the community: men, women, children and dogs. An old report described the chase clearly: 'Hotter and faster the running became, until at last the poor beast, entirely exhausted, was brought to bay, and despatched with the bull clubs.'

This was barbaric, of course, and many onlookers were disgusted. One historian put this well when he wrote that, 'Persons of a baser sort flocked in from all the neighbouring villages'. The event was held at Stamford. Then, in 1833, the Society for the Prevention of Cruelty to Animals stepped in and prosecuted, but the indictment failed. Five years later the local military were sent in to stop the event; in 1840, a petition was put to the Home Secretary stating that the practice would stop if the army were not sent for. The bull-running stopped soon after that, one of the last memorials to our national cruelty to animals.

⚜ BURGHLEY HOUSE HA HA ⚜

Many a pub quiz will ask what a 'ha ha' is. The answer is a 'sunk fence or ditch' (from the French *ha ha*). There have been ha has since the Norman era, and one survival is the ditch at Parkside Farm near Dover, which was part of a deer park made by Bishop Odo.

The great Elizabethan mansion of Burghley House was home of William Cecil, Elizabeth I's Lord High Treasurer. Before the mansion, there was a manor house on the site, and before that, a monastic retreat. The wonderful edifice was built and designed by John Thorpe, and the house has 145 rooms.

Later, in the age of 'Improvement' – the late eighteenth century and Regency years, when wealthy people were busy landscaping their country estates – along came the famous Capability Brown. In a period of over twenty years on the Burghley project, he created a lake, a bridge and the ha ha.

The Great Seal of Henry's daughter, Queen Elizabeth I. Burghley Mansion was built during her reign. Note the addition of the fleur de lys, and the two tiny hands stretching out her cape from either side.

One of the most famous signatures in English history: the elaborate handwriting of Elizabeth I.

The idea behind a ha ha is to make a visual illusion, but it also has a very practical use: the ditch prevents animals from going beyond the physical boundary. The idea was that, as Horace Walpole wrote in an essay on gardening, 'The contiguous ground of the park without the sunk fence was to be harmonized with the lawn within; and the garden in its turn was to be set free from its prim regularity, that it might assort with the wilder country without …'

Although the ditch at Burghley surrounds the enclosed lawns, to the eye it seems that, as Walpole noted, the wilder land without (outside) is seen as part of a continuous vista.

❖ BURIED ALIVE ❖

Today, we are used to the showmanship of David Blaine, who works in the tradition of the great Houdini, performing feats of extreme human endurance; this activity is now something that attracts national headlines. But Lincolnshire has its own star in this area of record-breaking: Emma Smith was buried alive for 101 days in a coffin 10ft below ground in September, 1968.

Houdini stepping into the crate that was to entomb him beneath the waves at New York Harbour in 1912. (Library of Congress, Prints & Photographs Division, LC-USZ62-22464)

In a feature commemorating that feat, the *Skegness Magazine* recalled in 2008 that Emma emerged into the light and told the press, 'I've proved a woman can do anything a man can do.' She was barely able to walk but was wearing a fur coat and sunglasses as if she were a movie star. She said, 'There were times, I admit, when it was difficult to go on. I thought about my husband and my children and I was very lonely.'

Obviously, there was a good deal of mental stress involved in her ordeal. At one point she felt that the roof of the coffin was bulging; her imagination was playing tricks on her. Emma had a button to press for emergencies – and it was pressed, but by mistake. But everything worked out fine, and a massive crowd was waiting for her when she was disinterred. She was examined by a doctor, who pronounced her to be very well.

Emma wanted nothing more than a hot bath after such deprivation, and she was taken to a hotel for that treat. The whole enterprise was done to raise money for charity. She kept a journal, but there seems to be no record of what happened to that; surely it would have made for interesting reading.

Lincolnshire folk soon celebrated the achievement. A correspondent to *Lincolnshire Life* magazine pointed out that Emma's achievement was not the only feat of endurance that Lincolnshire can boast of in the records. The writer noted that in Grimsby, the Grimsby Youth Orchestra had played Mozart's *Eine Kleine Nachtmusik* non-stop for longer than it had ever been played before, and also enjoyed telling readers that some butchers from Scunthorpe had produced the longest sausage on record, stretching to 3,124ft.

The challenge of being buried alive goes on. As I write this in 2011, Lincolnshire psychic medium and exorcist Ian Lawman, famous for the television programme *Living with the Dead*, has been buried alive to raise money for the charity looking after wounded soldiers from Afghanistan. He was in a coffin large enough for him to turn around in but not to sit up, and existed on tablets and water only.

Ian practised meditation to help him survive, and no doubt called on his spirit guide to help him to succeed. He did not consciously go for Emma's record; for him it was a test of his endurance, and a way to raise money for a very good cause.

C

⚶ CAISTOR GAD-WHIP ⚶

Ethel Rudkin, the authority on Lincolnshire folklore, investigated the traditions of the gad-whip. She spoke to an old lady in 1931 who explained the story of the ceremony that was done each year in Caistor:

> Every year on Palm Sunday a man would come from Broughton with a new gad-whip and he put a silver penny in the purse that was on the end of the thong – he used to keep the silver penny on purpose for the job – then a bit of wicken tree was bound round the whip-stock and that was done because the lad who was found on the 'Undon Hills was caught by the master at 'Undon and threshed with a branch of the wicken while he died ...

She then went on to say that the Broughton man stood by the north porch of the church and cracked the whip three times inside the church. The old lady said, 'The whip was taken to 'Undon after that and they do say there were twelve gad-whips in the garret at 'Undon and now there's not one left in 'Undon or Caistor. Mr McLane did away with the gad-whip crackin.'

The gad-whip story has origins clouded in mystery, but it is a Palm Sunday custom. This began when the estate of Broughton sent someone to crack the gad-whip while the first lesson was read. The whip was folded up as the man moved away to sit down. He then returned when the second lesson was read. According to the tradition, there have to be thirty pieces of silver in a purse tied at the upper end of the whip. The man would then kneel before the vicar, wave the whip three times and stay until the end of the lesson.

Clearly, the purse and silver are all about Judas Iscariot, but why was there a whip? The explanation given in Chambers' *Book of Days* is that it 'refers us back to the old procession of the ass, and the gad-whip of Caistor is the sole surviving relic.' A gad is a goad – for driving horses, so it fits with the 'procession of asses' tradition.

The tradition in Caistor was linked to land tenure at Broughton. When that particular holding ended in 1845, so did the gad-whipping.

⸜ CAREBY SANCTUARY KNOCKER ⸝

The word 'sanctuary' means 'inviolable' – beyond reach. The right of sanctuary, which would protect someone on the run from justice, developed in Saxon times, and by the Medieval period there were two versions of it. Ecclesiastical sanctuary had existed since the Saxons and became such that if a person was within a certain area of the church then they could not be taken. There was also secular sanctuary, which was basically obtained by having a royal grant.

If a person reached sanctuary, he could, in a period of forty days, take an oath before a coroner to confess a crime: he could be banished, but would not face the death penalty.

The special sanctuaries, made by royal charter, included Durham and Beverley. In those places there were people present all the time, ready to help troubled arrivals at their doors. But the system could be abused, as Henry Walker explains: 'In the fifteenth century the sanctuaries were frequently violated by ruffianly mobs; the claimants were no longer safe, and many were dragged from their refuges and murdered or otherwise maltreated.' In 1623 they were abolished.

In the early years of the institution, sanctuaries had knockers so the fugitive could summon help, sometimes when the seeker of refuge was being hotly pursued by the law or by enemies. There is a fine example of such a knocker on the south door of Careby Church near Little Bytham, and this dates from the fourteenth century. The figure in the centre of the building is St Stephen, sleeping, while two lizards seem to whisper in his ears, telling him that the Devil

Sanctuary knocker at Durham Cathedral. (Photograph by John Illingworth)

himself is near. The Christian message is clear: the Devil is always likely to work on you, even when asleep, when defences are down.

Tradition has it that a dent on the knocker is actually an example of a secret sign relating to the infamous Inquisition.

⚜ CLAY'S LIGHT ⚜

Halton Holgate is a mile away from Spilsby, described by one traveller in late Victorian times as 'a pleasant well-built village.' In 1881 it had just 499 inhabitants. It has a great deal of charm – but it also has the story of Thomas Clay. Over twenty years ago a local wrote to *Lincolnshire Life* magazine to ask about the story of Clay, and she referred to her disappointment that she had 'heard the bell toll for many residents', but had not seen Clay's Light.

The local tale is that this light warns of an imminent funeral. Thomas Clay was a man who lived alone by the 'Fen' – a mile away from the church. He was the churchwarden in the years 1658, 1661 and 1662, and apparently he would walk to church for service in the evening every Sunday, but he would not use the road, walking over rough ground instead. He asked that his own coffin be carried on that difficult route.

Halton Holgate church, where Clay was churchwarden. (Photograph by Richard Croft)

Thoughtfully, he left some cash to pay the unfortunate pall-bearers to do this.

Understandably, the general feeling was that such a task was a waste of time and so he was taken by road instead. But on the evening of the day when the funeral was to take place, a light was seen moving on the churchwarden's favoured route to church; the light then settled on the church tower. Since that day, the story goes, when someone is to pass away the light shines out over their home.

The village has another tale, told by a writer from Haxey in the 1980s . He wrote that there was a ghost at High Farm and that it could have been 'exorcised by the fire that destroyed the farmhouse.' The writer says:

> Just before the turn of the century, the little hunchback who was troubling the foreman and his wife … gained widespread notoriety. My parents, who were living in Manchester, read of this in the national papers. By a strange coincidence, they went to live in the small farm close by. In my childhood I often heard High Farm called the 'Ghost Farm' but none of us ever saw the ghost …

The place was something of a tourist attraction back in the late nineteenth century, but no hunchback sightings are recorded.

Halton Holgate certainly seems to be a place where unexplained occurrences happen. Research has, so far, not uncovered the truth behind the story of the hunchback and the burned farm, however.

⚜ CONINGSBY: MORE THAN AIRCRAFT ⚜

Although we always link Coningsby with the RAF, the famous Phantom jets and the Battle of Britain Memorial Squadron, it has many small mysteries. This rhyme is one of them:

> William of Coningsby came out of Brittany
> With his wife Tiffany,
> And his maid Maufrys
> And his dog Haridgras …

Its origin seems to have baffled scholars and historians. Coningsby is a place of old tales and anecdotes, myths and traditions. As with so many English locations, much of this is linked to public houses and taverns.

In 1884, when a picture was taken of the Black Swan, Coningsby had six inns and ten beerhouses.

The Leagate Inn has plenty of these tales attached to its history. Back in the late Middle Ages, the landlord lit a blazing beacon to help travellers on the dangerous fens to find their way. By the Leagate is Gibbet Nook Close, where wrong-doers met their end. They would have had their last drop to drink in the inn before they died; an engraving called 'The Last Supper' in the lounge refers to that. The inn has a former priest-hole – and, of course, a resident ghost. No one knows who the ghost, reputedly one Jack Cooper, was: but his spirit is said to sit in the inglenook of the fireplace. The inn is very old, incorporating vestiges of a former open hall, and has a seventeenth-century parlour block.

⚜ CONVICT TALES ⚜

Some of the county's most curious tales come from that dark episode in social history when thousands of people were transported to Australia, mainly in the first four decades of the nineteenth century. Most of these stories are very sad, but several are truly extraordinary. After all, Van Dieman's land and Botany Bay were not necessarily the end of the line.

The strange tale of William Wright, born in 1792, is a rags to riches classic. He was a staff sergeant in the South Lincolnshire Militia for seventeen years; then he led a gang of men working on turnpike stretches across the south of the county, but unfortunately they turned to crime. William went on the run, and hid himself away in a Folkingham brothel for two days, before being caught and then tried at Lincoln Assizes for stealing a gun and some iron. He was given a sentence of seven years' transportation and went to Tasmania, sailing on a ship called *The Lady Harewood* in 1829.

William's future was not to be as a rogue working on a chain gang at Port Arthur though. He made early release and by 1830 he was in a position of authority in Hobart, as District Constable and Overseer of Waterworks. Later he became Chief Constable of Melbourne, taking over from a man who had taken a bribe. He soon acquired enough money to buy a hotel and then had another built in a town called Bulla, where again he became Constable. As his commercial empire grew, he remembered his roots and called one of his properties, in Essendon, the Lincolnshire Arms Hotel. He died in 1856 at Deep Creek, after a happy family life.

Convict church built at Port Arthur,
Tasmania. (Photograph by Jorn Brauns)

In Sian Rees's book *The Floating Brothel*, she recounts the story of one of Lincoln's most celebrated convicts of the eighteenth century, Mary Rose, whose age at trial we do not really know. She could have been anything from sixteen to twenty. But whatever her age, the case fanned the flames of indignation around the city in 1788. The famous naturalist Sir Joseph Banks followed the case avidly, and a poem published in a local newspaper at the time has the lines:

> Twas then my wandering thoughts did bend
> To Lincoln prison dreary cell
> Where weeks and months without a friend,
> A ROSE, distressed, is forced to dwell.

What was Rose's crime? It began with a romantic elopement from Lincoln one night – the culmination of an affair with a young officer. Mary was only a farmer's daughter, so there were several reasons why a marriage would not have been on the cards.

Everything therefore suggested that young Mary was to be a 'fallen woman' if she could not be retrieved very quickly indeed. The search was on. Mary had a reasonable income, so she could have survived for perhaps a year even if her officer was penniless. However, only shame and dishonour waited for her if she pursued such a course. However, a sadder fate still awaited: for reasons which are not entirely clear, the officer fled. This left Mary, in her Lincoln lodging house, in some bother.

The landlady, a Mrs Kestleby, saw that there was some money to be had from this situation and shopped Mary for a supposed theft. Off went poor Mary from the magistrate to the prison to wait for the next circuit judge. There was a good turnout at the trial, as there were two murderers due to appear – and, of course, an attractive young woman. Mary could offer nothing in her defence and the course of events was frighteningly speedy.

Mary, along with some local housebreakers and thieves, was sentenced to be taken to 'parts beyond the seas' for her crime.

Mary was in gaol in Lincoln for eighteen months before any wagon arrived to take her to a ship. During that time her family brought her food and clothes, but time went on, and her situation began to look desperate indeed. Then Mr Banks began to take an interest.

Banks was involved with the colonisation of New South Wales, and a garrison had been founded and developed at Sydney Cove by the time this affair with Mary was in process. Banks did everything he could to have Mary taken to join this settlement, even paying out pocket money for her. Mary, for her part, did want to go there. Basically, the colony needed more women. It was that simple. Mary was an ideal candidate and so she went.

Her story reads like a Hollywood drama at times; it could also be a piece of fiction from Daniel Defoe. But the fact is that Mary Rose was a Lincolnshire girl who had this incredible adventure. Looking back at the story now, one wonders why the case even got so far. On the other hand, William Morris, a young man from Fleet 'was charged with feloniously stealing a horse... and a pony' and was transported for life. Here was another man with no powerful friends. Mary, with some income and a farming family, was in a better position, but could still not overcome the challenges and obstacles involved in the legal system of her time.

COY HE WAS NOT!
✢ HELPRINGHAM SUICIDE CASE ✢

Back in 1829, when times were really tough in the agricultural counties, a certain Francis Coy, a pauper in Helpringham, felt aggrieved. He took against the parish officers, feeling that he had been badly treated by them. But his vendetta was highly unusual. He did not walk into the church and commit mass murder or even attack the vicar. No, Francis just refused to do any kind of work at all. He told anyone in authority who accosted him, 'I've always conquered the parish and I always will!'

From somewhere he hatched a very odd plan. Something in his eccentric mind told him that if he took his own life within the church, then the place would have to be shut down for a year and a day. He may have found that strange myth in some old chap-book. Francis then told the whole village of his plan, and went ahead to hand-pick his pall-

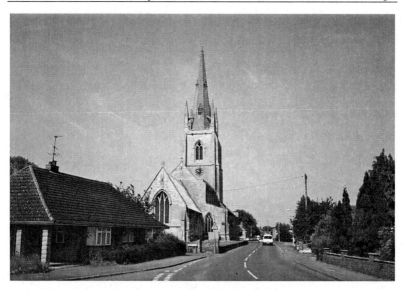

Helpringham and its church. (Photograph by Richard Croft)

bearers. He even gave the barber an advance payment for the shaving required on his dead body.

Naturally, this odd story went around the area and the parish authorities found out. The clergyman commanded the church gates to be locked up every day after use. But nothing could stop Francis. He climbed the walls and went to the porch, where he hanged himself. The coroner at the inquest found that the dead man had been of sound mind, so he had committed the crime of *felo de se* – suicide. He was buried on the night of the 5 June that year, and the church never had to close, not even for a day.

⚜ DANIEL LAMBERT ⚜

There have been many 'fat men' used in cheap shows and entertainments through history. Some, however, have become local or even national celebrities. But in most cases, famous or not, the unfortunate person had to live by means of their strangeness and maximise the potential for earning in zany shows and circuses.

Lincolnshire's Daniel Lambert is one such local celebrity, known for his largeness. He was born in Leicester but is buried in Stamford. Daniel was growing quite normally until he was twenty, and then some kind of medical ailment brought about immense weight gain; he weighed 32 stone in his early twenties.

With this kind of individual, the actual events get entangled with myths. There are stories of him attacking a bear with a stick, preventing it from killing a dog. Then there is the apparent loss of his job in the local gaol because he was too large to do the work. But one thing seems sure; he had to earn a living by being stared at. He was quite an attraction in London and also toured around the land, asking a fee merely to be seen.

Lambert was a very keen enthusiast for field sports; before he gained all the weight he was active in hunting and riding, and he was well-known as a dog-breeder. He had begun quite an adventurous life when young, going to Birmingham to work as an engraver. But by 1801 he was forty stones in weight and, as was commented at the time, six men would fit inside his waistcoat.

He had manners and pride, always insisting that men removed their hats when they visited. His most extraordinary visitor was surely Jozef Boruwlaski, who was only 3ft 3ins tall. They provided great entertainment together; at one time

The famous Daniel Lambert, and his rival heavyweight, Mr Bright.

Boruwlaski said that one of Lambert's sleeves would provide enough material to make a coat for himself.

After taking lodgings at the Waggon & Horses Inn in Stamford, Daniel Lambert sent a message to the *Mercury* about some handbills for his tour, and he asked a printer to go to him. He saw the printer and sorted out the order, then went to bed. After a night's sleep he got up, started to shave, and then collapsed and died.

He was buried in an elm coffin, built on wheels so it could be moved rather than carried; the challenge was to get the coffin out of the building, and to do that, a window and wall had to be demolished. He was then buried in the grounds of St Martin's church. It took half an hour for twenty men to pull the coffin to the grave. His gravestone is inscribed:

In remembrance of that PRODIGY in NATURE
DANIEL LAMBERT,
A native of LEICESTER:
Who was possessed of an exalted and convivial mind
And in personal greatness had no COMPETITOR.
He measured three feet one inch around the LEG
Nine feet four inches around the BODY

And weighed

FIFTY TWO STONE ELEVEN POUNDS!

He departed this life on the 21st of June 1809

AGED 39 YEARS

As a testimony of respect this stone is erected by his friends in Leicester.

❧ DEAD WIFE TALES ❧

Some tales in local tradition and in folklore tend to appear in counties across the land, and one of these, told in Lancashire and Yorkshire as well as in Lincolnshire, concerns the body of the dead wife and the hard-headed farmer. Martin Hughes recounted the Lincolnshire version a few years ago, locating the farmer in question as living at a house called Frog Hall near Coningsby.

The farmer was coming home late after work, when he saw a coffin being carried on a cart. He asked the driver who was the corpse.

'Mean to say you don't know?' the driver asked.

'Well, of course – how am I supposed to know?'

'Well, you should… because it's your wife in there!'

The farmer said that she was quite well that morning when he left home. He said, 'I'm sure she's not dead… just open up and we'll see.'

The coffin was taken home instead of to the graveyard – and sure enough, the wife was not dead. In the dark of night her voice was heard asking for a drink of water: and so she came back into normal life.

Another version of the tale is that the husband is taking his wife's body in the coffin, on a cart, around a tortuous road, with bend after bend, and at one really severe bend, the coffin cracks into a fence and the wife inside the coffin calls out for help. The farmer, after settling his irregular heart-beat, opens up the coffin and the couple embrace. They go home and live together till the day she really does die. Then he takes her to the graveyard – by another route, of course!

❧ DE VALERA ESCAPES FROM LINCOLN ❧

Visitors to the city of Lincoln would never be aware, unless they were suddenly taken very ill, that there was a grand and formidable Victorian prison close to the centre; it stands opposite the County Hospital, dominating Greetwell Road with its long, rounded-topped walls and castellar gatehouse. Opened in 1872, it replaced the old Georgian prison which was inside the castle grounds. In that long history, there have been very few escapes from Lincoln. George Brewer escaped in March 1943, to be recaptured within twenty-four hours, and in 1966 a man escaped using knotted bedclothes. But by far the most notorious escape was that of the future Taoiseach of the Irish republic, Eamon de Valera.

It was an amazing story, hitting the national headlines, and *The Times* reported the bare facts the day after – 5 February 1919. 'Hue and cry at Lincoln – Eamon de Valera, the Sinn Féin M.P, for East Clare, with two other Irish prisoners, escaped from Lincoln gaol some time between half past four o'clock yesterday afternoon and nine o'clock in the evening.' Tall and distinguished, de Valera had been a key player in the Dublin Easter Rising, being captured and imprisoned afterwards, and after spells at other prisons, was sent to Lincoln with other Sinn Féin men.

De Valera was a scholarly type, a mathematician. One of his friends at college was Charles Walker, and I have been told of a time much later in de Valera's life when Walker's text books were given to 'Dev' on a day when the famous politician invited Walker's daughter and grandchildren to tea. It says a lot about the man that he was so welcoming, but of course, his life was full of contradictions and puzzles (what politician doesn't have such complexities?). He was born in New York but raised in County Limerick by his grandmother; he was later educated at University College, Dublin, joining the Gaelic League in 1904 and the Irish Volunteers in 1913. He was involved in gun-running at Howth the year after, and commanded the third battalion of the Dublin Brigade in the Easter Rising of 1916.

Before ending up in Lincoln, he had been put in Kilmainham jail after the Rising and there he expected to be shot, writing this note to Mother Gonzaga at Carysfort Convent in Blackrock, where he was a maths teacher: 'I have just been told that I will be shot for my part in the Rebellion. Just a parting line to thank you and all the sisters… for your unvarying kindness to me in the past.' But he was reprieved and lived to see the inside of several other jails in his long career.

He escaped from Lincoln with two other men, John Milroy and John McGarry. The description given of de Valera says a lot about him: 'aged 35, a professor, standing 6ft 3ins and dressed in civilian clothes.' The report neatly summarised the fact that tracing the men was going to be virtually impossible: 'A close search has been made all over the city, but so far as was known at a late hour last evening the escaped prisoners had not been found.' They were not the only escapees from the Sinn Féin ranks: four men escaped from Usk prison the week before.

De Valera had been arrested in the 'round up' of May that year, stopped by detectives as he went home to Greystones in County Wicklow. He was then taken across the Irish Sea to Holyhead. The forecast by journalists at the time, that he would make his way back to Dublin and 'arrange for a dramatic reappearance in Irish politics', was quite right.

How did they manage to escape? Lincoln prison fronts Greetwell Road, but behind it at that time was merely open ground, beyond the rear exercise yards, and to the left, along the road heading out of Lincoln, there were merely limekiln areas then. The escape was arranged so that full use could be made of the vulnerability at the rear. There was still constant supervision to overcome, however, and of course, they needed a master key.

A committee of Irishmen was set up to arrange the escape, and they selected a number of men to do the job. The focus was the small patch of ground used as the exercise yard; it was surrounded by barbed wire, armed warders watched in the daylight hours, and an army unit came to patrol at sunset. Sensibly, the first decision was to decide not to try a direct assault – a rush – as there would have been a gun fight. The next plan was to start by finding a way to communicate with de Valera. The answer was to use the Irish language. An Irish prisoner who was working on a garden plot in the jail sang a song, and the words gave de Valera the planned breakout. The second time a song was sung it was to direct de Valera to have an impression made of the key that would open the back gate. Today such methods would not be possible, but then there was more work outside and so there was a degree of vulnerability with regards to the system. According to one report, the key impression was made by snatching a key from a warder to press into a bar of soap, but this seems very unlikely, given the fact that the key would be on a chain and always snapped into a belt-purse when not in use. Far more likely is the theory that a prison chaplain made the impression in soap or in a bread paste. The first two keys made did not fit anyway, and then the third model worked well.

The impression was wrapped in brown paper and thrown over the wall. Then came the hard part: de Valera would be able to walk through from the main prison building, but there were the sentries to consider. They would have to be distracted, and the way to do that was to use female allure. Two girls from Ireland were used, as the local girls may well have split on them. The *Lincolnshire Echo* reported that they were 'attractive, vivacious Irish girls, both university graduates, and they were directed to flirt with the guards.' On 3 February, four cars were sent around the country around Lincoln to create decoys and keep the police occupied; then, at dusk, the Irish girls began to work on the guards. They lured them away from the prison recreation area and the Sinn Féiners then cut through the barbed wire and waited for de Valera to appear: he did, after some initial trouble. The key broke in the lock from the outside, as Michael Collins, who had come to lead the attack, tried to force it, but luckily de Valera, from the inside, managed to force it out.

They had to move very quickly, because Collins and Boland drove straight to the city railway station and caught a train to London. But de Valera and the others split up and drove to Manchester.

The conclusion given by the prison authorities about the escape was that it was facilitated by the fact that the internees were allowed to associate much more closely than ordinary prisoners, and were not subject to such close supervision. Shortly afterwards, Terence MacSweeney was released on parole from Lincoln as his wife was seriously ill.

In their time in Lincoln, the Sinn Féin prisoners were treated very well. The journal of the prison doctor records his examinations of them, and there are regular entries in that book. For a long period, several were on hunger strike, and the doctor records his comments about each one, as well as noting their weight. Paradoxically, one of the prisoners put on weight during the hunger strike – a footnote to history perhaps not widely known, and a fact that adds a darkly humorous dimension to those troubled times.

⸙ DUNSTAN PILLAR AND THE HELLFIRE MAN ⸙

Nocton is a village six miles south-east of Lincoln, one of a cluster of villages across a moor which is on the border of fenland. Anyone walking or driving past this area would never suspect that it has connections with several people who were important and charismatic figures in English history, notably from the late seventeenth century through to Victorian times. But of all the characters linked to Nocton and Nocton Hall, Sir Francis Dashwood has to be the most intriguing. This vibrant, energetic man was many things: clubman, politician, traveller and, above all, a dilettante.

The story of Dunstan Pillar is perhaps Dashwood's most famous tale. That story begins with the time when Dashwood married the widow of Sir Richard Ellys. Although he was born in West Wycombe and was educated at Eton, Dashwood had interests and connections across the country and was a tireless visitor and socialite. He married Lady Ellys in 1745, three years after she lost her first husband at St George's, Hanover

The ruined shell of Nocton Hall. (Photograph by Richard Croft)

Square; but he was not a Londoner, and in fact, has been written about as a 'Lincolnshire blood' of his time.

Sir Francis moved in high circles, such as national politics (he was member for New Romney in 1741) and academia, being elected a Fellow of the Royal Society in 1746, and even taking up the post of Chancellor of the Exchequer. In the record books, he is as much Lord le Despencer as he is Dashwood. All this suggests a kind of duality, a double life, and in fact that is not far from the truth.

In 1745 he adopted Lincolnshire as his home and the focus of his attention was the building of Dunstan Pillar, completed in 1751. It was to be a land lighthouse, as the broad area of heath land was dangerous for travellers; the area was not farmed at that time. The pillar was 100ft high and it had a lantern placed at the top. It functioned as a lighthouse until a storm damaged it in 1808. Tradition says that the project began with a wager that a stone column of that height could not be constructed on a narrow base. If this is the case, then Dashwood won his bet.

It would not be entirely wrong to call Dunstan Pillar a 'folly', but we should recall that in its time it was far more than a solid pillar with a lantern on top. It had a staircase inside, and it was meant to be developed into a much more spacious building. Whether it actually did ever become more than the pillar is doubtful, but the plans were for several rooms to be added, including dining rooms and kitchens. One report in 1836 does talk about 'four little buildings'.

After the damage, a carving of George III was placed on the top, made of a substance called coade stone. During the Second World War this was taken down, as it was seen to be dangerous for low-flying aircraft. The statue of the king now stands in the grounds of Lincoln Castle. When it was placed there, it was a challenge to the ingenuity of the restorers, as no one knew how to make coade stone; the factory making that stone had closed in 1843. In more recent times, Christopher Cleere has worked out what the manufacture of that stone entails and one day the other parts of the carving may be assembled.

Dashwood, always a sociable man, was very much the kind of rebel individualist that the early eighteenth century produced; it was an age of extremes in culture and in sport. The aristocrats gambled as well as spending money on art collections and on giving their sons the luxury of the Grand Tour. But although Dashwood is linked to the founding of the Hell-Fire Club, the Brotherhood of St Francis of Wycombe, he was also a member of the Lincoln Club, which met at the Green Man Inn on the heath. It comes as no surprise, really, as Dashwood had several Lincolnshire connections. His cousin was Francis Fane of Fulbeck and he had close friends in the Spalding Gentlemen's Society. But the ties with Lincoln, rather than the south of the county, were what he desired. At that time, there were around a dozen similar clubs in the county, and each had its own character and aims, mirroring the nationwide growth of radical and liberal clubs, which were interested in fun and entertainment as well as good fellowship. The Lincoln Club owed its existence to Thomas Chaplin of Blankney, who was a nephew of Thomas Archer, founder of the Dilettanti Society. Their meeting place, the Green Man, was given a long club room and all around the long table were busts of the members.

What is hard to imagine now is the nature of the whole place at this time;

Dunstan pillar. (Photograph by Richard Croft)

The south-west view of Lincoln Castle, engraved at the end of the eighteenth century.

the Green Man meetings, the speeches, drinking, gambling and good company, alongside a pleasure garden built around the pillar. This was an amazingly beautiful place, compared by some to the famous Vauxhall Gardens in London. Memoirs of local people say how attractive this was, commenting on the bowling green and other retreats and peaceful spots. After all, this was the era in which wealthy men with country estates were paying poets to live in artificial grottos built on their land. It was an age of landscaping and 'projections' of design in all areas of aristocratic life and culture.

Dashwood would often be away from home; he was a man with a diverse range of interests. One of his acquaintances (featured later in the story of George III's mental illness) was Dashwood's keeper at times when he wanted someone to take care of Dunstan: this was Dr Francis Willis. Basically, he acted as Dashwood's agent. He certainly needed some help there, because the Lord of Nocton was full of schemes and ideas. The Hell-Fire community was ultimately based on the imaginary abbey invented by the French writer, Francois Rabelais, in his *Gargantua and Pantagruel* (1532). This was the Abbey of Theleme, and the motto was 'Love, And Do What You Will.' The first Hell-Fire club had been formed by the famous rake, Lord Wharton, around 1720. Dashwood's own motto in this respect was, 'Taste the sweets of all things.'

It was said of Dashwood at the time that he had 'the staying-power of a stallion and the impetuosity of a bull'. He liked to act and to posture. In parliament he was notably direct and blunt. He wanted risk and danger, excitement and escape; he found this in a Hell-Fire club that was already going well, the George and Vulture in London. But he started on the road to sensual freedom and amorality when he took an interest in the Society of Dilettanti. Literally, the word means, 'those who take delight or pleasure'. This group met on the first Sunday of every month at a tavern in Covent Garden. There was a love of meaningless ritual embedded in this fun: a member called a Very High Steward used to walk with an image of God fashioned in silver, tied around the neck.

There was also a more serious side to the Dilettanti: many of the members were lords and they had travelled widely. It was made a stipulation for entry to the Society that one had to have visited Italy. That says a lot about their taste. They yearned for something different to the stodgy conservatism of their elders, under the safe, steady regime of Sir Robert Walpole. Instead they craved a wasteland of classical statuary and a few orgies to go with it.

Dashwood was drawn to the East as well and became a member of a Hell-Fire club involving a special 'divan'. The special attraction of this was that you could dress up; this was a major part of the appeal of the clubs. At the Thatched Tavern in St James's Street, members could enjoy the divan, dressed as moors; of course, it was not too difficult to provide a 'harem' for entertainment. This was the age when attractive young women who wanted a career as a mistress or as a high-class escort could be toasted and treated at a club meeting and the wealthy young men (and older lounge-lizards, no doubt) could provide a good income for the *parvenu* young women entering high society.

E

⁜ ECCENTRICS OF THE SHIRE ⁜

Lincolnshire has no shortage of characters, though it could be argued that England generally seems to create strong personalities and people with odd habits and behaviour. Sometimes we might use the word simply to describe someone who is mildly eccentric, while at other times it identifies a person either with an obsession or with extreme tastes or hobbies.

One of the classic templates of the Lincolnshire eccentric has to be Henry Welby. His name is linked with Goxhill, and so he has put that small place firmly in the history of memorable folk. Welby was born some time in the mid-sixteenth century, and we know that he died in 1636, so he had a long life, and perhaps his diet had something to do with that.

He bought the estate of Goxhill from Lord Wentworth and then travelled, before settling down. However, it seems that there was a confrontation with a half-brother called John, who tried to kill Henry after a disagreement about moral behaviour. He married a niece of the great Lord Burleigh, but his wife died soon after and Henry decided to withdraw into seclusion. This was, according to an earlier historian, around the year 1592. He withdrew to live in Grub Street, London.

For over forty years, Henry lived the life of a recluse. He had three 'private chambers' which he lived in, and never ventured out of them. According to one story, 'While his diet was set on the table by one of his servants – an old maid – he retired into his lodging chamber, and while his bed was made, into his study, and so on till all was clear.' No one saw his face in all those years except his maid.

One of the most remarkable aspects of his hermit's life was his diet. He lived mostly on oatmeal boiled with water and a herb salad. His special treat was the yolk of an egg, the soft part of a loaf of bread, and beer.

Henry Welby, the
'Grub Street Hermit'.

❧ ELECTION TALES ❧

Elections in the nineteenth century were invariably the scenes of riots and fights. After all, local passions ran high when strangers came in to stand for their seat and take on the locals. The local man might also be a hard landowner with entrenched conservative views, or perhaps a magistrate who would be hated by many. Allegiances were strong and found aggressive outlets whenever there was a sniff of something dramatic and sensational on the wind. In Lincoln in the 1820s there had even been a murder associated with a candidate. Then Grimsby had several riotous elections, the worst coming in 1862; violence broke out again twelve years later.

In 1862, just eleven years after the Yarborough Hotel had been built, things were improving for the town. A new railway had been constructed and the hotel had been built by the great Lord Yarborough, who was chairman of the Manchester, Sheffield and Lincolnshire Railway Company. Then, in that fateful year for local politics, a riot started there, resulting in much of the interior being wrecked; the hotel had always been a favourite spot for local businessmen to meet – in the smoke room usually.

Yarborough Hotel, Grimsby, scene of a riot. (Photograph by David Wright)

Trouble had been expected and police were standing by earlier in the day, brought in from Hull. But what caused the trouble was something familiar in local elections at the time – outsiders brought in to help organise a campaign, in this case towards the Liberal candidate, Heneage. Two men from Liverpool were brought in to do this, and as they were being given a grand meal, the enemy arrived. The hatred seems to have been directed towards the two voters inside. Even their own sisters were in the crowd, shouting that they would 'tear their eyes out' if they supported Heneage. According to a contemporary account, the women were 'violent blackguards', determined to cause a fight. Thanks to their provocations, matters escalated and the mob attacked, turning the Yarborough Hotel into the site of a hellish brawl. Many thought that the fifty policemen from Hull acted so extremely that they aggravated the situation, but whatever the cause, the result was chaos and destruction. Sixteen police officers had been inside the building, but they thought that discretion was the better part of valour and they beat a retreat. This supports the view that it was left to the Hull men to sort things out and that they did so with too much vigour.

When normality was more or less restored, arrests were made and four men were given prison sentences. Naturally, after the storm and the election itself (at which Heneage lost) the loser was certain that his enemies had planned everything; a stool-pigeon called Hopkin was located and found to have voted against his employer. In the days well before the Secret Ballot Act of 1872, this could happen. The tale was that the poor man had been plied with drink and put onto a London train.

In 1877 another election riot damaged the Royal Hotel. In May 1877 there was a by-election. After walking out of the House of Commons, the MP John Chapman died; he had been ill since the 1874 election and now his demise opened up new campaigns. Heneage (who was to become member for Grimsby later), declined the offer of a place on the railway board – always the marker for the 'railway seat' as it was often called. It was to create something of a mess and so the trouble followed. The 'railway candidate' became Watkin, after his approaches to Heneage and to George Morland Hutton had failed. But Watkin had made moves: when two railway secretaries arrived in Grimsby with Heneage, they saw people on the platform with banners reading, 'Vote for Watkin'. The trouble this time was not as severe as in 1862, but there was certainly a fight that did some damage at the Royal. The police, now more informed and organised, kept trouble to a minimum. Alfred Watkin won, and Edward Heneage's turn was to come in 1880. In the meantime he had other duties: he was appointed one of the sheriffs for Lincolnshire in 1877. He was also MP for Grimsby from 1880 to 1886, as Liberal, and again in the years 1886-1892 and 1893-1898.

⚜ FIRE STATION SPECTRE ⚜

In the course of researching some Lincolnshire ghost experiences, I answered a phone-call one night, and was told the tale of a homely, restful work-break being torn apart by unexplained movement, unnerving noise, and a mysterious evening guest. This was certainly something unexplained and an experience that has lived in the mind of an old man to this day.

Back in 1947, when men were leaving the RAF and looking for work, one of the attractions was to enrol in the Fire Service. But those who started work at the Gainsborough station in Lord Street might have regretted the decision. Former firemen have told me eerie tales of working in that place.

The old appliance room was all that was left of the original building, and it was the custom of the officers to go through the ritual of essential tasks before sitting down to socialise and listen to the radio. The last job of the day was to lock the side door. There was an external alarm bell for the general public to ring if an emergency arose.

One officer recalls that, during the social time, when their kit was hung on the wall, one man was making a model galleon, and the largest piece of wood, about a foot long, was thrown inexplicably across the room, slamming into the opposite wall. Then footsteps were heard outside and approaching the side door. Everyone heard the footsteps as they were talking and they seemed to come into the building. The Sub Officer accused a man of not locking the door, but they all walked to see what was going on.

The loud footfalls came into the main room, and then slowly padded along the stone slabs of the corridor. The officers followed, in awe of what they had heard. On the steps they went, across a yard and up some steps to a locked store-room which had dangerous substances in it. The officers were, naturally, shaking with fear. Their heads turned, and they felt the floor shake slightly to the sound of these ghostly footsteps across the room and slowly up the stairs. Then the handle on the door was rattled.

Big, strong men, fearless against the terrors of fire and smoke, shivered with fright that night, roused from a friendly game of dominoes and the homely sound of the radio, to witness something uncanny.

But it seems that Lord Street has even more ghostly activity. One man who lived behind a greengrocer's shop three doors along from the fire station remembers some mysterious events there. He talks of a long passage leading to the outside doorway, where he and his wife started to hear loud rapping on the door. Local police would sometimes call in for a cuppa, so they had a chance to talk about their concerns. When the door was opened, however, there was never anyone there.

One night, when the banging was particularly loud, events played out differently. The man opened the door – and to his horror, the noises continued, all around him, even without the door to rap on. This became a regular part of life in the house – and to make things worse, there was an upper floor where people often they heard steps ringing out in the empty room. The man eventually nailed battens across the stairs to block exit and entrance to the upper floor.

It seems that Lord Street and the nearby Casket Street had (and maybe still have) their share of beings from the other world, and one in particular who likes to walk into dangerous places. People asked about these experiences have no explanation from history, but there is much still to be unearthed about the footfalls in the fire station.

⁂ FLOOD FOLKLORE ⁂

There is an old legend in Horncastle that the town will be flooded whenever the vicar of that parish is changed. The pattern of floods in the area followed that story in the years 1919, 1959 and 1981, when floods followed a new vicar's arrival within a year of the event. In 1960 there was a truly terrible inundation. October had seen prolonged Atlantic depressions over the whole country and the rainfall was utterly engulfing; it is, so far, the third wettest October since records began in 1910.

On 7 October that year, as Paul Simons wrote in *The Times* in 2010, 'Despite the wet weather there were many warm days. October 7 was especially hot and muggy, and a terrific thunderstorm brewed up in the heat over Lincolnshire, which erupted into a spectacular downpour.

River Meadows,
Horncastle, the flood
plain of the River Bain.
(Photograph by
Tony Atkin)

Horncastle had seven inches of rain in just three hours — a record still standing as I write this in November, 2010.

In the town, streets went under water. One man, Fred Holmes, went missing and the press reported that there was a widespread search for him, and several elderly people had to be rescued by police officers. In one street a man was swept off his feet by the water and was rescued by some quick-thinking man on a boat who pulled him to safety. At one time the water was as high as the tops of phone boxes, and the bridge, which was part of the Lincoln road, was at one time totally submerged.

People from Mablethorpe and Grimsby came to help; there were over 500 people drafted in to help with rescue work. The Red Cross opened a first-aid post and a rest centre was made.

As meteorologists point out, Horncastle is in a valley where two rivers meet: they both burst their banks and so the floods formed very quickly indeed. Folklore, people must have thought, should be heeded. But we have had a flood in the town in 2007 and there was no vicar installed in the previous year.

⚘ FLOWER POWER ⚘

Henry Flower, back in 1840, was man with a savage tongue. He expressed his dislike if he felt it, and on one occasion he found himself in the national press — for the wrong reasons. His bad language put the village of Gedney on the map, but not in a good way at all. It was a sorry state of affairs, because he let loose his feelings against his vicar, for whom he worked as sexton.

The vicar of Gedney had been involved in some correspondence with the Bishop of Lincoln concerning the Wesleyan Methodists, who at that time were growing fast across the county, with their chapels proliferating and their esteem very high. But then Mr Flower attacked the vicar, T.S. Escott, and had to then apologise. This grovelling expression of remorse actually appeared in *The Times*:

> I, Henry Flower, do hereby ask pardon of the Vicar of Gedney, in that I have without cause most grossly slandered and abused the sacred office which the Vicar holds as an apostle of Jesus Christ, and have falsely accused him through a desire of revenge, or being led away by the malice and instigation of the Devil, having said that he had been in a state of intoxication, which I know to be utterly untrue; and also having asserted that he evilly entreated the wife of his bosom, which I likewise confess to be a most imaginary falsehood...'

It has to be imagined that Mr Flower walked through the streets wearing sack-cloth and maybe wearing a hair shirt, so deep was this contrition. But what about the vicar? How did he respond? He would have been expected to show Christian charity.

He made sure that his pardon was also printed in *The Times*, and he made his good character clear by stating that the matter would not go to a church court, as it normally would have done: 'as far as concerns myself, and considering his contrition, I condescend, in the plenitude of forgiveness, to stay proceedings in the ecclesiastical court against one who is far advanced in years, and who, if I were inexorable, must end his days in a prison.'

That was laying it on a bit thick. The old man was hardly likely to lie in jail for a few nasty words. But the case shows that in rural Lincolnshire, the English language, in all its glory and grandeur, was alive and well. The old man probably only cursed under his breath after that – and the vicar surely kept to a drop of sherry and no more.

✥ GEORGE III AND A ROW AT THE ASYLUM ✥

In 1792, William Goodwin of Earl Soham wrote in his diary:

> April 2. The Queen of Portugal has been in a state of lunacy for several months; Dr
> Willis, a clergyman who attended the king, was called for, who found 47 medical
> men and 54 priests surrounding her majesty. All these he routed, directed her little
> medicine and no religion, recommending asses' milk, a better regime and good air,
> and the queen mended is said to be recovered.

Dr Francis Willis and his two medical sons were clearly national celebrities.
Willis was 'the Lincolnshire mad doctor' with a court nickname of 'Dr
Duplicate' because he combined twin careers of doctor and priest. He
and his asylum at Gretford both figure prominently in the history of
psychiatric therapy in the county, but Lincoln itself was a major centre of
this work from the first asylums to the Bracebridge Lunatic Asylum, south
of the city.

The first Willis was called in to treat George III in 1788 and he had
a lot to offer, though he had no idea what was actually wrong with
the king: he was simply 'mad' and doing irrational things, whimsical,
cruel and threatening. We now know that the king was suffering from
porphyria, after research done by Dr Martin Warren on a strand of
George's hair found in a museum. The hair was found to have 300 times
the normal level of arsenic; but the diagnosis of porphyria was made
after research done on the king's case history: notably his dark red urine.
This made porphyria the certain cause of the 'madness.' The disease
causes seizures and cramps, and sympathy for the poor royal sufferer
must emerge when we reflect on the treatment he had most of the time:
blood-letting and leaches.

What we now know is that King George was using a wig powder in
the eighteenth century, and skin cream, both usually laced with arsenic;

he was also being given antimony as part of the treatment, and this too contains arsenic. His medicine was causing his insane moods and violence.

Francis Willis was a singularly impressive man. A courtier described him as 'open, honest, dauntless, light-hearted, innocent and high-minded.' He had worked in Lincoln, in 1769, and had acquired such a reputation that Oxford gave him a medical degree. He may have looked ordinary and unremarkable, but he was a force to be reckoned with.

He opened his first madhouse in Greatford in 1776. He was a clergyman, and therefore an amateur in medicine, but his eldest son, John, was medically qualified. John lived until 1833, and another son, Robert, treated the king until 1810, so there was a dynasty. We have an account of his Lincolnshire asylum written before he treated the king:

> As the unprepared traveller approached the town, he was astonished to find almost all
> the surrounding ploughmen, gardeners, threshers and... labourers attired in black coats,
> white waistcoats, black silk breeches and the head of each '*bien poudre, frise et arrange.*'
> These were the doctor's patients, and dress, neatness of person and exercise being the
> principle features of his admirable system, health and cheerfulness conjoined...

In other words, Willis did not accept the usual treatment of using restraining jackets and keeping patients in dark rooms. Private madhouses were not legally licensed in England until 1774, and what often happened was that managers exploited patients and took money from their families, for no real treatment. William Hogarth's print from *The Rake's Progress* (1735) shows the rake on the floor at Bethlem Hospital, London. He is surrounded by various lunatics, apparently without guidance, restraint or supervision, and he scratches his head in a frenzy. Images like this perhaps convey the usual methods used at the time. Then Dr Willis and others like him started the revolution in psychiatry.

When he was called to Kew to treat the king, he first achieved dominance by eye-fixing, out-staring the patient, letting him know who was in charge. The king resisted this but finally lost the struggle; from then on it was a healthy regime, with exercise and diet, and also the threat of the straitjacket if he became unruly: it was the threat only, except in rare instances. He was also kept seated for long periods in a special chair, and at one time, as he had been saying insulting things about Lady Pembroke, he was strapped in the chair and lectured. Both Willises were meticulous in the discipline they imposed, and John Willis kept a diary, recording details of symptoms and behaviour, noting such things as a 'whitish tongue' and blood in the urine.

King George gradually came to fear and respect his physician, after at first despising him. George had at first said, 'You have quitted a profession I love, and you have embraced one I most heartily detest.'

Willis replied, 'Our Saviour himself went about healing the sick.' And George had a bitter answer ready:

'Yes, but He had not £700 a year for it, hey!'

It was literally to be a battle royale, but Willis won. In early 1789, the king began to return to health.

Dr John Willis was to attend the king again in 1811. He and his father had been well paid for their work, receiving £20,000 from the king, and the same sum from the Queen of Portugal. John was given £65 a year for the rest of his life; he died in Lincolnshire, at Longhills, in 1833.

In a year in which an Asylums Act was passed to begin more regulation of these places, Dr John Willis set up the hospital we now call The Lawn in Lincoln. This beautiful building had first been planned after a bequest of £100 from a local surgeon in 1803. But it had been financed from public funds, and designed by Richard Ingleman. The Lawn had its first visiting doctor in 1820, Edward Parker Charlesworth. He was to play an important part in the history of psychiatry, together with Robert Gardiner Hill, who arrived in 1835. The Lawn was to be maintained in this role of mental health treatment for 160 years, closing in 1985.

Charlesworth was married to the daughter of a doctor from Horncastle, and had gathered plenty of experience as a doctor at Lincoln County Hospital before he began visiting work at The Lawns. There, he was faced by the accepted treatments of restraint and suppression. Patients were sometimes tethered to their beds or to posts. The Lincoln Lunatic Asylum, as it was called, had room for fifty patients, but there was no finance for a doctor. The families of the patients would have to pay Charlesworth on his visits. It would be money well spent. As the nineteenth century advanced, awareness of mental illness gradually increased, and in the early 1840s there was open debate in the press about how the mentally ill should be treated, with the issue of 'mechanical restraint' at the centre. Lincoln was at the heart of this discussion, and Charlesworth's presence was one reason why this was so.

Charlesworth's involvement in the hospital steadily grew; he became a Governor, and he tried to promote the kind of thinking about patients that would lead to separation of people according to their specific illness. In 1828 he wrote a letter to the Board of Governors confronting the issues of restraint and supervision. His words were simple but powerful, as in his account of the atmosphere: 'The former courts of the asylum, small, damp, cold and cheerless, without sunshine, ventilation or prospect, as also the dangerous association of the convalescent with other patients, evils publicly advocated… are a striking instance of this position.'

One particular event was perhaps formative in bringing about change: a patient called William Scrivinger had died after being strapped to his bed overnight. There was a complaint from the parish officers that Scrivinger was 'placed among several of the worst patients.' He had not been closely supervised, of course. His death had been caused by strangulation.

It took a confrontation with the director, Thomas Fisher, to bring about any radical change. The letters between them were acrimonious and certainly ungentlemanly for the time. Finally Fisher left, resigning before a general meeting that would have brought shame and embarrassment to him; he was succeeded by Henry Marston.

In the early 1830s, Charlesworth, with the support of Marston, began to make Lincoln an enterprising and exemplary centre for the treatment of the mentally ill. Many of Charlesworth's ideas could now be implemented, particularly in enforcing a closer and more professional supervision of people at risk within the walls. The amount of restraint exercised was steadily lessened. By 1839 there was a general acceptance of a non-restraint policy. There were to be more rows between physicians and Governors, but by 1853, when Charlesworth died, there was little doubt that his achievements had been truly admirable. His statue now stands at a corner of The Lawn grounds: that has to be a tacit acknowledgement that, whoever else was involved in debates and reforms, Edward Parker Charlesworth stands as the man who made things happen.

As for the poor, they had their turn when Bracebridge Asylum was opened in 1852. If we want to see evidence of the kind of reforms and new thinking that Charlesworth helped to bring about, we can note that the new asylum had a farm covering several acres; it had recreation rooms and laundry; and that during the winter months, there were regular entertainments provided for staff and inmates. This was a new world indeed in psychiatry. In 1898, there were almost a thousand patients there.

Previously, only the wealthy had been able to find openings for their mentally troubled relatives where they would be humanely treated and supervised, as the Poet Tennyson did in 1840, when he gave £1,000 to Matthew Allen, the doctor who treated John Clare, and who also treated Tennyson's brother, Septimus.

⚜ GIBBETS ⚜

Writing in 1926, W.J. Rawnsley discussed these grotesque reminders of a barbarous element of the criminal justice system of the past:

> The name gibbet hill or gibbet post is not uncommon but I doubt if a single post remains. Eighty years ago some still held their ghastly record. My uncle, Edward Rawnsley who was born in 1815, told me once that he had passed one with a skeleton hanging in chains, as he rode from Bourne to Wisbech.

The posts may all have gone, but trees were also used. A farm in Normanby, by Spital, still has a tree referred to as 'the gibbet tree' according to the website, *Lincolnshire Gothic*.

The word comes from the Old French, *gibet*, meaning a stick. They were usually a long pole on which the body of a hanged killer was left out for the birds to peck at and eat. The idea was that such a gruesome sight would be a deterrent to any potential criminals who might pass by. An Act of 1752 ordered the hanging of bodies in irons, but earlier, after the Monmouth Rebellion of 1685, Judge Jeffreys had ordered the bodies of rebels to be gibbeted along a certain route.

The first known case of a man's corpse being gibbeted in the county is that of John Keel in 1731. He was a woodcutter from Bardney with a large family, and he liked a drink or two. One night, in a drunken temper, he started to create bloody mayhem on his wife and children, using a hooked hatchet. His wife was stabbed in the throat and chest. He was tried at Lincoln and sentenced to hang by Lord Baron Page. A publication on the event at the time tells us that the gibbet on which his body hung was at Hoffam Walk at cross-roads (where gibbets were often placed) between Mucton and Louth.

An old print of
the gibbet.

⁓ GRANTHAM DISASTER MYSTERY ⁓

Train crashes are always big news, but in 1906 Grantham had a terrible disaster on the railway that is perhaps most remembered for the baffling mystery surrounding the circumstances of that horrendous event.

The locomotive in question was the night-mail to Edinburgh, having twelve coaches; it was an Atlantic design, number 276, and it was due to stop at Grantham at eleven at night to drop the mail. Everything depends on signalling systems, of course, and on this fateful day the south box, covering the entry to the station, was fine – showing the 'caution' light. But north, the controls showed 'danger'.

The atmosphere was just as a grainy documentary would show it – dank and miserable weather, but not so bad that lights could not be seen. Everything was going as it normally did as the staff waited on the platform, the Post Office staff with the inspector. When they saw the train coming, they realised, horrified, that the 'run through' train flying towards them at top speed was the one with the mail on board. It should definitely not have been steaming through Grantham at high speed.

The signalman at the south box was the one person who saw the footplate, and later on, when he had to speak at the official enquiry, he stated that he had seen the driver and the fireman doing exactly what they normally did: looking ahead whilst standing in their usual places. But the train had sped into the stretch where the 'danger' sign was showing, and crashed to its doom in the darkness. The majority of carriages were hurled over a bridge and down into embankment. Amazingly, only the last three sections of the train were unaffected. *The Times* described the horror:

> There is a curve in the Nottingham line, and the rule is for trains to pass through at a very slow pace. This train rushed through, rocked on the rail, dashed into a wall, and then, after proceeding in this fashion for some distance, broke into three pieces… The engine toppled over and buried itself.

The mystery is why and how this happened, of course. The death toll was high: twelve passengers, one mail sorter, and the engine crew all lost their lives. But at the enquiry, nothing was confirmed or understood about the events of that momentous night. Statements about whether or not the brakes were used were contradictory; there was so much extreme damage to the controls that it was impossible to ascertain a narrative of the events leading up to the crash. One person swore he saw the driver and fireman

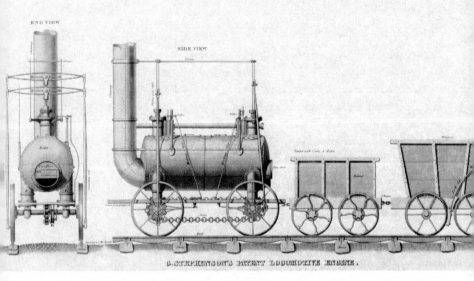

Stevenson's Rocket, which also caused a horrible and tragic accident – on its very first outing. (Libray of Congress, Prints & Photographs Division, LC-USZ62-110386)

fighting at the time. It is stunning that so many different testimonies were given, and if there was a fight that caused the disaster then that would be very hard to believe. Some years ago, writer Robert Tyrell suggested that this was fanciful and was indeed imagined, perhaps with its source in a novel called *La Bête Humaine* by Emile Zola (in which two railwaymen fought over an affair one had with the other's wife). At the end of the enquiry no resolution was given, but Mr Tankerville Chamberlyne wrote to the press to suggest that the cause was obvious: 'the train was timed to stop at Grantham, and… no train so timed had ever failed to do so before. Thus not the slightest provision for safety in case of the failure of the mechanical brakes, a breakage in the engine preventing the driver from shutting off steam at the proper time.'

One theory was that the regulator, used for shutting off the steam, had malfunctioned. The writer summed up what should always have been done: 'The points should not be touched until the train had pulled up at the platform.'

There were other lines of thought. One suggestion was that a resolution had been passed at a meeting of the Amalgamated Society of Railway Servants: 'That this branch strongly sympathize with the killed and injured in this shocking calamity at Grantham and we are strongly of opinion that enginemen generally are not allowed sufficient time for food and recuperation from long journeys.' They did not blame any member of staff, and simply pointed at the Great Northern Railway as being negligent.

Maybe the latter explanation was right, as all projected technical explanations were not to be proved. The mystery will go on.

⁕ GRAYINGHAM: MURDER AND MYTH ⁕

This story could begin with a myth rather than with the historical facts, as far as we know them. This was featured in *The Scunthorpe Evening Telegraph* in 1954, and the feature was headed, 'Legend of Gate where no Grass would Grow.' The piece describes a local legend around the villages of Kirton-in-Lindsey and Grayingham, that the grass in the corner of a field called Leonard's Field would never grow. Even today, this is a very peaceful place; at the junction of a B road and Grayingham lane, there is little more than a farm track.

The feature reports that, 'It is a fascinating yarn that Kirton folk still tell to their children and grandchildren. For the story springs from the town's most notorious murder.' There are many features in the actual narrative that help us to understand why there should be a myth around this. What is essentially a tale of two drunken friends falling out leads to much more, and the events tell us a great deal about the nature of murder investigations at the time.

A few days before Christmas, 1847, Joseph Travis and his friend Charles Copeman went for a drink or two and they were seen arguing. On the Sunday morning afterwards, Copeman was found dead in the field, in a ditch, with his head severely bruised, his throat cut and, as the first report stated, 'quite dead'. There had been a very vicious attack, of such extent that even the man's dog was found with him, stabbed and bruised. On Christmas Eve the local press delivered a detailed account of the discovery of the body:

> On Sunday morning at about nine o'clock, as John Whelpton, a labouring man, was proceeding to Kirton along the bridle path leading from Grayingham, his attention was attracted by a dog sitting on something by the road-side which … he discovered to be a human body with the face downwards and the dog sitting upon the back. Two other men came up directly but none of them dared approach.

Whelpton did some elementary observation as a
constable was called by another man, and he noted
that there were footmarks discernible, matching the
dead man's boots, from the Kirton direction and
another set of footprints from the east side, joining
the victim's. Not far from the body there were obvious
signs of a desperate struggle, and also a wallet containing two
half crowns, a shilling and a six-pence piece.

When the law arrived and a crowd had gathered, the body was
moved and there was the face of the man all bystanders would have
known. There was a deep wound on the left of his face; a slash had cut
across the jugular. There was a cut below one eye and another down the
side of the whole face to one side. The nasal bone was broken and there
was a severed ear and a gash from the ear to the throat. The attack had
been savage and brutal. The conclusion was that, as there was no blood
on the man's breast, the wounds had been inflicted when the victim was
down on his back.

It was assumed that there had been more than one assailant and several
men were arrested and questioned in Gainsborough, about ten miles
away, on Monday. A handbill was circulated with a reward of £100 for
the apprehension of the killer. However, local suspects were arrested on
flimsy grounds based on hearsay and conjecture. Some individuals were
reprimanded simply because they were known trouble makers. Joseph
Travis, however, emerged as the main suspect, albeit on circumstantial
evidence. Travis was twenty-four, a joiner and cabinet maker, the son of
a local farmer. *The Lincolnshire Chronicle* reported on 31 December that
Travis was 'respectably connected' but that he had 'for some time led a
most dissipated life and has lost considerable sums at card playing.' When
questioned, Travis, according to one contemporary reporter, 'gave a
statement replete with gross contradictions.'

Travis was arrested and charged with wilful murder. This first emerged
at the inquest in Kirton, so it only needed a coroner's warrant to have
him taken to Lincoln Castle. One of the county coroners, C.H. Holgate,
had presided. There had been an initial inquiry on the Monday at which
several witnesses had been questioned at length, and then the inquest was
adjourned until the Wednesday. Travis and Copeman had been drinking
at the Greyhound Inn in Kirton, with some other men. There had been
an altercation and Travis and Copeman very nearly came to blows. But
most of the men moved on to continue the binge at the Red Lion, and
it was noticed that Travis stayed alone at the Greyhound. It is easy to

imagine the situation: Travis had been humiliated; he was very drunk and also without cash. Then he had been abandoned by his drinking friends. Copeman had plenty of money on him. Travis confessed to the crime, but he escaped the noose.

Strangely, forty years later, when there were some attacks on the road at Broughton, a few miles away, a key witness was one Edward Whelpton. As for the Copeman and Travis families, they were still there a decade after the murder; by that time Daniel Copeman, the victim's son, was running the place, and Joseph's parents, George and Elizabeth, were still keeping up their business. Their occasional meetings must have been very strained.

The truth about the legend of no grass growing at the corner of Leonard's Field is that a roadman at the time, whose task was to cut back the roadside vegetation, realised that there was intense public interest in the local murder and kept the scene of the crime open and flat, so that passers-by could satisfy their curiosity about the circumstances of this brutal killing.

Today, the Red Lion is only hinted at by the presence of Lion Passage, a small thoroughfare leading from the central square of Kirton. The market square does not easily evoke those wild times when navvies turned out to fight. But much of the village is still as it was then and the geography of this notorious killing can be comprehended by a short walk around the streets and lanes. As the local historian H.A. Fisher has explained, 'Even in Lion Passage leading from South Cliff Road to Market Place, named after the Red Lion pub at its eastern end, had cottages, the steps of which can still be set in the ground.' In other words, in 1849 people were huddled in small living spaces around there. Whatever went on in the street, with a brooding, malevolent man like Travis hanging around on a corner, and the loud and inebriated mob filling the square would be seen by plenty of local inhabitants.

❧ GREESTONE STAIRS PHANTOM ❧

The guide on the official Ghost Walk around Bailgate will tell you with relish about the epicentre of paranormal activity that is Greestone Stairs. Local folk will tell you of a hand that darts out to grasp your ankles as you innocently stroll down the stairs towards the centre of the city. That is the local tale, but far more unsettling are the sightings on the stairs. These range from the experiences of a young woman to those of a churchman.

Greestone Stairs, epicentre of paranormal activity. (Photograph by Richard Croft)

Close to the stairs is a building that used to be a tithe barn and then a hospital. Today it is used by the University of Lincoln, but the fact that it was once a hospital may explain the recurrence of a ghost of a young woman seen on the stairs. She has been seen standing on the stairs with a baby in her arms, although in most cases her figure is not standing actually on the stone. Accounts of this say that the air is chilled and a feeling of 'time stopped' somehow emanates. Then the young woman and baby appear, as if the spirit is aching to convey some kind of pain associated with her troubles.

There have also been sightings of a priest on the stairs. People have apparently seen a man in the apparel of a churchman from the Georgian or Stuart period walking up the stairs. He tends to move upwards and then fade into a wall. Hearsay would have us believe that there was a suicide there at one time, and certainly that would be a suitably dark venue for such a horrible event.

Most eerie of all are the hands that are supposed to grab the walker's ankles. That may be hysteria, as the quiet stairs can create an irrational inner fear if the walker is alone, going steadily and carefully down that very steep incline. All I can say is that on one of my own visits there with a group of other people, a woman sensed that she was held on the arm by something, and that only stopped when she screamed out for help, thinking she was being attacked.

⁂ GRIMSBY SPIES ⁂

In the years before the First World War, England was subject to fits of spy mania. People were seeing German spies everywhere and anyone with a German name was potentially open to suspicion. The newspapers were full of lurid accounts of supposed spies on trial. Even the writer D.H. Lawrence, who had married a German and was living in Cornwall, was thought to be involved in sending signals to German submarines, though nothing was ever proved.

It is in this atmosphere that Grimsby had its own episode of spy activity. A Swedish man called Ernst Olsson was convicted at Lincoln Assizes on 17 June 1915 for trying to gather information that would constitute an offence under the Official Secrets Act of 1911. The Act and all its provisions sprang from years of uncertainty about how to change and streamline the military intelligence of the realm. After the Boer War of 1899-1902 and the dynamic growth of the German Empire in Africa, Britain was confused about how to plan and improve its actions against espionage at home. The German intelligence system, initially naval with Admiral von Tirpitz in charge, was certainly organising a spy-ring here, and the new MI5 department under Colonel Vernon Kell had been impressively effective against these spies, who were looking for information at dockyards.

Every sea port was vulnerable and Grimsby was no exception. Olsson was charged with looking for information about the defences and sea power elements as observed in the Humber. Another man of the same nationality who was living in Grimsby, Erander, had been working with him. On 16 March, a conversation between these two had been overheard and reported. In this interchange they said that in the coming war the Germans were sure to win and then Olsson revealed that he had some German friends in Rotterdam. He said that they were trying to extract some information about the naval and military situation in Grimsby. He was heard asking Erander for that type of information. They were being tailed and clearly it was not difficult to listen in on their talk, because a week later they were listened to again and this time Erander was asked if he had made a decision about passing on such information. Erander's actual words were noted. He said, 'Life is sweeter than money to me; I have been in Grimsby fifteen years and I have been treated like a man, and it would be the last thing I should do.'

That second conversation was the foundation of the accusation against Olsson; he had said that some of his friends were Germans with big

German liners laid up at Rotterdam; he was condemned. On 7 April they met again and he repeated that statement. He said that his friends over the North Sea were working hard to obtain the military information. Then, stepping up the talk to something more definite and alarming, he spoke of a fleet of 130 or 170 Zeppelins that were ready to fly over the sea to drop bombs on England when the weather was right. When he actually moved on to talk about his occupation as a U-Boat pilot he was really in trouble. After that Olsson wandered into more dangerous territory, with a discourse about him being set up in a small boat on the East Coast 'with petrol and provisions to supply the Germans at sea.'

Lipson Ward, defending the Swedish man, managed to argue the last statement away, defining it as irrelevant to the charge. At his appeal hearing in February, the final statement was successfully removed as indictable, but the second ground for appeal – that the trial had been prejudiced by a card found on his person – was judged to be admissible. The card had been a summary of naval signalling, something that it was argued was generally available and which he had owned since 1911.

The judge, Mr Justice Horridge, allowed the charge about the card to stand and the Swede was cross-examined. Everything the defence could come up with failed and Olsson was sentenced to four years' penal servitude. The Official Secrets Act, something people were still trying to fully understand, had clearly laid down that penal servitude was the punishment for 'communicating or intending to communicate secrets to a foreign state or an agent of a foreign state.' Olsson's talk of friends in Rotterdam had been his downfall.

In the same year, a certain Carl Muller had been executed by firing squad for spying; he also had friends in Rotterdam and he had sent letters to them written in German, about shipping dispositions. Robert Rosenthal met the same fate after sending coded details to Germany about shipping in Hull.

The efficiency of the team of officers led by Kell in London was astonishing, and it stemmed from an overheard conversation on a train in which two Germans were discussing a letter from Potsdam, which was about British preparations for war. Grimsby played its part in that successful counter-espionage ring and the detectives, busy at the port, were part of a team working at all major ports. As far as Olsson was concerned, there seems to have been an element of fantasy and wish-fulfilment in his ramblings to his friend. In fact, the words spoken by his friend are very important in understanding the depth of support for counter-espionage among civilians; after all, the man Erander had been welcomed and respected in his adopted country and this was a buffer against the blandishments of his friend, who was convinced of German superiority.

As a writer to the paper had said in the same year, discussing the German spy-scares, 'Altogether different is the position of the spy in time of peace. In some cases he is merely an adventurer working for money; he is then corrupt and it is his business to corrupt others.' That is exactly what Olsson was trying to do, but he was too bold and careless. He never would have made a James Bond. But there was a larger-scale development well into operation: the spymasters in Germany had in fact organised a widespread operation. In 1907, a man called Widenmann had taken over as naval attaché in England, and he had three agents ready and waiting to serve him.

One of these agents managed to start an association, linking his work with a company called the Argo Steamship Co. who were based in Bremen. The agent, de Boer, would act as the agent in Hull and Grimsby, working for the organisation in Germany running espionage, the Admiralstab. The plan didn't really work and de Boer was neglected by his masters for some time.

What this does tell us, however, is that characters like Olsson were around the ports, ready and willing to be approached and enlisted by men like de Boers. We have to wonder whether, on a day when Olsson was hanging around and up to no good, he met either de Boers or one of his cronies. Certainly something fired him with enthusiasm for Germany and its imperial designs. Still, thanks to the beginnings of MI5 in the establishment of the Secret Service under Captain Vernon Kell in 1909, the German spy ring never succeeded. It did not stop spy scares such as this one in Grimsby, but it did make the men involved in them easier to track down. Methods of reconnaissance were so sophisticated by 1911 that it was almost impossible for an amateur like Olsson to achieve anything – and with his lack of tact and tendency to talk and brag he was doomed to failure from the start. By the last phase of pre-war activities by aspiring German spies, one of their leaders wrote, 'For the time being the matter [of spying] works on no account.' That never stopped the irrational stories of Germans hiding in cupboards and the terrible destruction of property owned by anyone with a German-sounding name, which still happened regularly in the war years.

H

❧ HARLAXTON ❧

Harlaxton Manor overlooks the attractive Vale of Belvoir, and the house, at one time known as Grantham Castle, was built between 1837 and 1854 by Gregory Gregory, an art collector. It was sold in 1937 to Violet van der Elst, a woman who spent many years campaigning for the abolition of capital punishment. Then, between 1948 and 1965, the Jesuits ran the place. There is no doubt that Mrs Van der Elst was a powerful presence at the manor. She used to hold séances to try to make contact with her dead husband. These séances would be held in the library, a place described by one writer as 'sombre … with its twisted pillars from Italy and huge windows which were once covered with black velvet curtains.'

Harlaxton Manor in 1880; a view from Revd Morris' *Country Seats*.

In the Jesuit period, there were frequent and unnerving disturbances at the manor, and there was an exorcism. A recurring ghostly tale is that of a young woman with a baby. Apparently many years before, a young nurse had a baby on her lap by the fire, and she went to sleep, letting the child fall helplessly into the fire, burning to death. The scene for these appearances is the ante room, and in that spot there have been all kinds of strange events. It is said that people have arrived there for the first time saying that they heard the cries of a baby. Rumour would have us believe that a hole in the chest of one of the decorative cherubs on the wall is something that testifies to the sad happening there.

The noted ghost-hunter Peter Underwood once went to Harlaxton to give a lecture to some students, and he followed the talk by sleeping in the Clock Room, another paranormal location here. One of the students told Underwood of having terrible dreams, one time waking to see, 'what looked like a sub-human face close to his own, and sometimes, during the quiet of the evening, he had glimpsed a dark-robed figure in the room.' Other students, part of the American University of Evansville, spoke of seeing that same robed figure and of witnessing other shapes and figures in the rooms. But Underwood ends his account of the visit on a positive note: 'Never shall I forget the first time entering the massive door, and Joyce and I finding ourselves alone in the sombre, shadowy, echoing stone entrance at Harlaxton.'

It could be that these unholy spirits were stirred from their repose by the questionable doings of Mrs Van der Elst, but the death of the child is supposedly something that happened in the Clock Room, and that tragedy had nothing to do with her séances – as far as we know. The questions remain, of course.

Mrs Van der Elst is surely one of the unsung heroes of Lincolnshire. She was so set against any kind of judicial hanging that she busied herself with leading demonstrations against the use of the noose. Her very large and posh car was often filmed being used as a road block and an obstruction by prison gates. If there was a hanging announced, she would be there stirring up trouble, and she wrote to every dignitary she could think of to gather support in her humanitarian cause. Eventually she wrote a book with an account of her campaigns and the stories behind the condemned people she worked for – and indeed prayed for. This work was *On the Gallows*, published in 1936. In it she reprinted letters from people who had refused to support her, including one from the Bishop of London.

The lady was always in the centre of controversy – and often in court. In 1936 she appeared before the magistrate in Manchester after refusing to stop her car during scenes following the execution of Dr Buck Ruxton. She told the court that an officer had said to her, 'You will get prison this time. We are going to have you medically examined.' Clearly, she had been in a ruck. A doctor who examined her the day after the Manchester demonstration told the court that she had two bruises on her hip – 'He suggested they were due to an act of violence.'

A year before that she had been robbed: a maid at her flat stole four pieces of carved Chinese ivory. A detective found these figures in her room wrapped in leaves. The maid said to him, 'I am fed up with all this and I will find some peace… if I have to commit suicide.' Poor Violet was always involved in affairs of this kind.

She was born Violet Dodge in Surrey, the daughter of a coalman and a washerwoman and, incredibly, she started as a scullery maid and then went into business, making her fortune with 'Shavex', a brushless shaving cream. She married a Belgian painter – hence her very exotic name. With her money she bought Harlaxton, but such was the intensity of her campaigning and her foray into politics that she lost her fortune and moved to live in a London flat. Happily for her, the year after her death, in 1966, the death penalty was abolished. Given her personality, we can well imagine that a ghost in Harlaxton is indeed her restless shade, still out to disturb the peace.

HARRY PRICE AND ⁂ THE BINBROOK BURNING MYSTERY ⁂

The great ghost investigator, Harry Price, was fascinated by unexplained fires, and one story, from Binbrook Farm near Grimsby, he linked to a poltergeist. There had been mysterious fires reported there between December 1904 and January 1905 and one report had mentioned a burning blanket in a room where there was no fire.

Price knew that there had been typical poltergeist disturbances at the farm; objects had been thrown around a room, noises had been heard and a young girl had been burned. Someone or something was tearing out the throats of the chickens in the yard as well.

Then the local newspaper got hold of the story and printed this report: 'A story that greatly dismays the unsophisticated is that of the servant girl, who while sweeping the floor, was burned on the back. This is how the farmer relates it: "Our servant girl, who we had taken from the workhouse, and who had neither kin nor friend, was sweeping the kitchen. There was a very small fire in the grate and there was a guard there… I suddenly came into the kitchen, and there she was with her back on fire. She looked around as I shouted, and seeing the flames, rushed through the door. She tripped and I smothered the fire out with wet sacks. But she was still terribly burned…" '

She was taken to Louth hospital. There, she told people that she had been in the middle of the room when the burning started. Regarding the chickens, it was later reported that, of 250 fowls, only twenty-four were left. The windpipes of the dead birds had been drawn out and snapped.

No less a person than Charles Fort made notes on the case, and he saw that there had also been a fire at Market Rasen where a fowl-house had been set on fire and destroyed. But the strangest aspect of this story is that, while the young servant was in the hospital, a man called Ashton Clodd, also a patient there, died due to burns he sustained after falling into a fire, just a few days after the farm fires.

As for Harry Price, he too had actually seen such a thing when he was young. He wrote that at a house near him in Shardloes Road, Brockley had suffered a fire. He explained, 'It appears that at about 5.30 on the afternoon in question, every curtain in the house blazed up in quick succession – first one side of the window, then the other. It was as if a trail of gunpowder had been laid in all the rooms…'

❖ HAXEY HOOD ❖

This has to be a contender for being Lincolnshire's most curious piece of folklore, and it has been a main event on the Isle of Axholme calendar for many years. Haxey is just three miles away from Epworth, the capital of the ancient Isle of Axholme, and the Hood game, an intriguing tradition that came about quite opportunistically, is focused on rivalry with nearby Westwoodside. Some folklorists connect the Hood with plough jags and there is a view that the boggans are linked in some way to ploughs, so that this could be a Plough Monday affair, but that seems unlikely. But first we need an explanation of the boggans and the hood.

The origins of the game go back in legend to the story of Lady Mowbray, who was riding her horse on a windy day when her red hood was blown off. Local men tried to retrieve it for her and they were twelve in number in the old tale. Lady Mowbray thought that it was all such fun that she gave thirteen half-acres of land to pay for this to be a custom. The numbers twelve and thirteen come into the game and the participants are the boggans.

For a week before the hood day, the Fool (there is always one) and the twelve boggans go around the villages collecting money and having a good time. They traditionally sing some standard well-known folk songs, the main one being 'Drink England Dry', with lines that relate back to the Napoleonic wars:

> For the French the invade us, they say they will try,
> They say they will come and drink Old England dry.

A writer in 1932 explained, 'In years gone by the Procession of the twelve Boggans, headed by the Fool, marched from Wroot to Haxey on the 6th. Look-out was kept from Haxey Church tower, and as soon as there was a first glimpse of them, the bells pealed out.'

The rough play begins when the hood is thrown after a speech by the Fool; then the Fool leads the crowd to the first half-acre and the first hood is thrown. Everyone runs after it. The boggans have to stop any man running ahead and crossing a boundary. One writer explains the rugby-like ruck that usually takes place in a field of crops:

> Then would one extricate himself triumphantly with the hood in his hand, and he
> in his turn would set off running with it, while the first holder pulled himself out,
> the sorriest, wettest mess you ever saw, hair, face, clothes all the colour of the wet,
> black earth that he had rolled in …

Another rule of the game dictates that if there is a local celebrity present (and of course there is) then he or she has to throw the second hood, made of leather. The celebrity had to throw the hood straight up into the air, and then this 'sway hood' is pursued and struggled for. The ultimate aim is to take the hood to the Carpenter's Arms in Westwoodside, where the landlord offers everyone free drinks.

All this seems like complete mayhem, with great risk of causalities, but one standard rhyme explains the limits:

Hoose agen hoose, toone agen toone,
If tho' meets a man, knock 'im doone
But don't 'ut 'im!

⚜ HIBALDSTOW WATER COLOUR ⚜

Many in this beautiful little Lincolnshire village have seen her as she walks across a landing or through a yard. She is the White Lady to the residents of the row of eighteenth-century cottages in Hibaldstow, and the only evidence they have of her existence in this life is a gravestone behind a fireplace.

There are four adjoining cottages, once inhabited by labourers working at a nearby dairy. I spoke to three people here, and all have seen or felt a presence in their homes. Some years ago, during renovations, the gravestone was found, and all it had was a name and a date. Now even that is forgotten as the stone was replaced behind the hearth and a new person moved in. But she walks and she has been seen.

In The White House, once a tavern and also a lock-up with a resident constable, the present owner saw her in the early hours of one morning last year. As he walked in the half-light across a small landing, there she was, looking at him. He describes a filmy shape, with a darker shade at the heart and a discernible face, sweet and lovely, seeming to look through him. There has been a séance and the people present were given the name 'Florry'. At other times, her figure has been seen but seemingly 'with no legs', so supporting the view that the development of the house, over the years, has meant alterations to levels on which people move.

The White House has also been a place of some poltergeist activity. Early one morning, a cabinet full of pottery and silverware shook and the only object to have been dislodged was one newly bought for an aunt – a high quality commemorative plate. Silhouettes of human shapes are often seen and, at times, the presence of a distinctive and repellent smell by the log basket near the fire has been noted.

Something about Hibaldstow (in Old English 'the place of Hubald') attracts spirits from the other side. In this same street there have been sightings of four different entities as they walk across the closely-knit back gardens. An old man with a pipe has been seen several times, and his tobacco-smoke is often sensed around the garden.

But most amazingly of all was my own experience of the watercolour that gives this haunting its name. I was taken to a small bedroom in which, the owner tells me, she has often heard movements and voices above her as she sits in the kitchen below. She took me to see this room, and as we entered she pointed out a watercolour to the right of the door. This was a Victorian painting showing a stone gateway surrounded by dark foliage, and to the lower right of this was the only light area of the picture, showing flagstones with moonlight upon them.

She then told me about the voices in the room, and her family's sightings of two men moving around the house. We spoke about this, and I was aware of nothing unusual, but then she asked me to look again at the painting. To my amazement, the picture was now suffused with light, as if colour had stolen into the vegetation as it would in the real world. I was stunned, and immediately lifted the painting off the wall, to look behind. There was no trick. It was as if the leaves and branches had been suddenly stroked by rays of the sun and night had turned to day. All I saw behind was a sheet of cardboard and the name K.E. Halket. I have not found this name in any reference work on Victorian painters.

I was told by the owner of the house that the painting was given to her by 'a Quaker lady' who said it would help her retain her faith. Apparently, the painting does these changes almost every week, but never when taken to any other residence.

Everything about this Hibaldstow tale is full of mystery: who was the Quaker lady? Who wanders around the back gardens of the cottages leaving the smell of tobacco? More intriguing is who the two men were in that back bedroom upstairs – men seen and heard by the daughters of the house. The small black cat that lives there seems unperturbed by these events, but who knows what inhabits that mysterious painting?

The houses are very old. The street itself has a sense of timelessness. All the stories of the atmosphere around the dairymen's cottages suggest a little world that comes alive in the dark, only 'alive' may not be the right word to use. More likely, there are creatures wandering the corridors and crossing the landings that were living beings many, many years ago and cannot leave the village today.

There is a long and intriguing history here, of the White Lady and of the watercolour. We may only have a clue if and when the hearthstone is dug out and there is a name. Meanwhile, she walks at early dawn and chooses to be seen at times, perhaps having something to communicate about that quiet lane in Lincolnshire where the small cottages huddle together, near a stables and a farm.

All I know is that I saw the watercolour change in front of me; I saw the dark landscape suffused with a glorious light that had not been there a few minutes earlier. If there is an explanation for these things, they defy science. My visit there was dominated by a black cat, a sense of being watched, and a small piece of canvas on a wall that appears to have defied the normal rules of what we call reality.

⚜ HORNCASTLE CHURCHYARD 'GHOST' ⚜

Back in 1922, Agnes Armstrong published a collection of tales from this area – arguably the most unnerving is her ghost story. She told the tale of a man called David Watson who was quite clear that he did not believe in what he called the 'white sheet' – a type of apparition. But he related how a skeptical friend called Bill came one day from the churchyard at Horncastle, terrified, and said, 'Well off goes I whistling up the big pad as bunk as you please, but when I got to the back of the church I soon altered my tale, for all of a sudden like from amongst the graves I heard a queer scraping sort of noise, and then my heart turned clean over …'

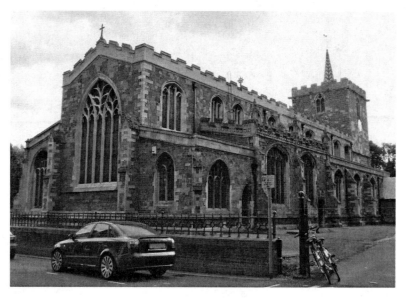

Horncastle church.

He said that he saw 'summat white lifting itself in and out'. He ran, saying to himself, 'Matthew, Mark, Luke and John, bless the bed as I lay on.' But the ghost stopped beckoning to the man and poor scared Bill said that the ghost 'groaned and groaned and I groaned, and you may depend that my hair stood on end with fright, and the ghost said, "Who are ye?"'

The poor man stuttered some kind of reply, but then realized that the ghost was a man he knew: 'I see'd it was nobbut old Jerry Jackson in a white slop, digging graves in the dark with a light.'

✤ IMPS ✤

Of course Imps and Lincoln will be forever linked in folklore as well as in the tourist industry. The imp has generated no end of stories, and in fact the curiosity in this tale lies in something generally found in folklore: the tendency for stories to create other, off-shoot stories. The origins become obscure and no-one really knows why or when many tales began. Even the word 'imp' is strange. It comes from the Latin *impa-impotus*, meaning a graft, as originally an imp was a shoot or scion, but it came to mean a taunting and mischievous child, little Devil or wicked sprite. In a recent BBC feature investigating imp stories, correspondents told tales never before heard, but the tourist postcards tend to concentrate on the one central tale.

In this story Satan sent an imp to Lincoln Cathedral to stir up some mayhem, because that is what Satan likes to do. The imp intended to wreck the angel choir, but when an angel made an appearance there was a scrap, and the nasty imp threw chunks of stone at the angel. In retaliation, the angel turned the imp to stone, intent on getting some peace – and the imp is still there today, in stone, in the angel choir.

However, there is another story of an imp, this time with medieval origins. In this tale, Satan sent two imps to perform some mischief. First they went to Chesterfield, where they put some weight on the spire so that it would go crooked and then they went to Lincoln, determined to destroy anything they could get their hands on. Again, the angel appeared to challenge them, turning one to stone, but giving the other one a chance to get away.

Lincoln Cathedral spire – which, unlike the example at Chesterfield, escaped the imp's attentions.

The interior of Lincoln Cathedral, drawn in around 1850.

Yet another account concerns the imp who was blown into the cathedral by strong winds. Finding himself in this solemn place, he started playing and dancing around excitedly, but just as he broke into a smile he got turned to stone – hence the mischievous grin on the statue. All the stories have something in common, but people who responded to the BBC website had other spin-off stories. One of the most intriguing revealed the rumour that if a pilgrim kneels in front of the saints' tomb and asks for the forgiveness of sins, an imp will appear at your left shoulder, reminding you to stay good.

⚜ ISAAC KIRTON ⚜

This is a Lincolnshire haunting from the doyen of ghost-hunters, Peter Underwood. In his autobiography, *No Common Task,* he relates a tale told by Sir William Pike, who was a member of the Huddleston family. The man in the tale, called Kirton, was actually a Huddleston and the story is from the Lincolnshire Fens.

In the early years of the nineteenth century, Kirton, who was a farmer with a strong presence in the Methodist community, was riding along an area between Crowland and Fosdyke Wash when the weather turned for the worse. He was still a long way from his destination when a frightful storm erupted, drenching him to the bone. There was no choice but to stop and find somewhere to sleep for the night. Kirton saw that there was an old inn quite close, a place off the beaten track, with traditional and very basic accommodation. He went in and asked the landlady for a bed. The author of the tale, Mary Huddleston, writing in the late Victorian years, relates that it took some time for Kirton to persuade the woman that he really was in desperate need of a bed and some rest.

She finally relented and led him down a long passage on the ground floor to his bed. He rested, but there were some locals having a hard drinking session that night and he could not sleep until they had gone. He read, and waited. Then, after midnight, he fancied he could lay down his head, but as he did so there was a rapping at the door. Kirton opened the door but saw nothing. Again, he lay down – and again came the knocking. To his astonishment, he opened the door and saw three men facing him. One man spoke for the three, saying that they were three drovers and that a few months earlier they had come through the village from a fair where they had made some money. According to Huddleston, this is what the drover said next:

> The landlord, who is a crafty man, coveted our gold and murdered us in our beds and buried our bodies in the back yard that may be seen from your window there. If you will come with us we will show you the exact spot, so that the dark deed done that night may be brought to light and justice done.

Kirton followed the men to the yard and they pointed to the spot where their bodies lay. Shivering with fear, the farmer then saw them dissolve and disappear before his eyes, but he had the presence of mind to stick his whip in the ground at the place they had located.

The next day, Kirton just had to find out if his terrifying experience had been a real apparition and resolved to find out if the burial place was really where the drovers were. He found a local man with a spade to go with him for a good payment, and the ground was dug, as Kirton watched. At first the man saw some clothing and soon after that he shouted that he could see an emaciated arm, then a skull. Soon the earth was removed and there were indeed three bodies down there.

The landlord confessed and was carried off to trial. He was later executed at Lincoln, or so Huddleston says. This is a good story, but unfortunately there is no record of a hanging at Lincoln for such an offence. He may have been hanged elsewhere of course, but that is unlikely.

❧ JOHNNIE OSBORNE ❧

Agnes Armstrong tells of one of Horncastle's genuine personalities in her collection of tales published in 1922. He was the kind of local man around whom anecdotes seem to generate, and Agnes knew that all local people reading her book would either have heard of him, or would have known him.

Johnnie, the parish clerk, was a general aide-de-camp to the vicar and his humour comes through in stories of his everyday duties, as well as in his nature. He is described as 'a clever man, and a good loyal churchman, usually speaking in a broad Lincolnshire dialect.'

A story that surely informs the world about his extreme character is the occasion when a widow and widower were being married. Though a new record book for marriages had just been beautifully bound ready for use, Johnnie brought out the old battered one. When the vicar asked why, Johnnie said, 'It's all right Sir, I keep t'other for the virgins. Owt's good enough for these second-hand do's.'

His letters also provide excellent entertainment; often they are of a practical nature, as in this request: 'Rev. and Dear Sir, The body of Thos ... has shown such unmistakable signs of decomposition that the funeral originally fixed for Thursday at 3 p.m. must perforce take place on Wednesday at the same hour.'

Johnnie comes across over the years as a figure similar to the butler Jeeves, who rules the roost and dictates by a mix of common sense and prejudice. He must have irritated people, as this story shows. He once called on someone holding a violin and saying, 'Please, I've brought this violin back. I borrowed it once.'

He had borrowed it forty years previously. We need men like Johnnie around today; the types who carry on as they are, regardless of offence or of how they might look to others. His strengths were clearly in his insouciance and his will to control matters as he deemed appropriate.

Thanks to Agnes Armstrong, his name did not recede into the oblivion of local memory.

⚜ JOHNNIE O' THE GRASS ⚜

Back in the days of superstition, and when many folk were short of money and could not afford to see a doctor or take other professional advice, the so-called 'wise' men or wise woman did very well. One of these was Johnny o' the Grass from Louth. He was reckoned to have special powers (they all were, of course) and according to John Ketteringham, these special powers are open to anyone who can hold three pewter plates 'one inside another, under a bracken fern, to catch the spores'. These spores are supposed to rise and pass through the plates.

The problem for the person who can handle these plates and deal with the spores, is that Old Nick himself will then appear and he will be riding on a pig. But the good news is that he will, if you haven't already run for it, make you a wise man or woman and give you extraordinary abilities.

Johnny o' the Grass was clearly someone who had met the Devil under these circumstances and so was very savvy. He was supposed to have ridden to a toll bar at Girsby Hall and was told that he need pay nothing because he was a man, but that his donkey had to pay the usual toll. Johnny's way around the problem was to turn his donkey into a man, so that it could walk through the toll with no charge. It then became a donkey again after passing through.

Johnny, man and myth, may well have had such powers, but clearly the locals would not dare to challenge him on that, for fear of being transmuted into some kind of animal perhaps.

⚜ JURY JAPES ⚜

Some of the county's most curious tales have come from the records of the assize courts. In the Georgian and Victorian years, the judges had a high level of power and were often notably eccentric and whimsical. Partly for this reason, their cases generated stories which are bizarre and sometimes puzzling.

Take for instance the events of December 1857, when Mr Justice Crompton presided. Before him was a poaching case, but there was a shortage of jurors. The jury foreman, Sir C.H.J. Anderson of Lea, said

Lincoln Crown Court, formerly the Assize Court. (Photograph by Richard Croft)

he was the presenter in a poaching case committed by four men on his own estate. He naturally applied to be excused duty and had arranged for another man to step in. Justice Crompton said, 'I cannot see how I can substitute one grand juryman for another after the charge has been delivered… I have never known such a thing before.'

His Honour was aware that having the knight and plaintiff on his jury could be seen to be a problem, as he wanted to avoid any impression from the lower classes that would reflect badly on the administration of justice. What was he to do? The only solution was to drop the whole affair and discharge the alleged poachers.

Then there was the strange behaviour of Mr Justice Maule, a notable character on the Bench, who in 1852 complained that there was no fresh air in his court and ordered all the windows to be opened. But there was no response, so he had a fit of temper and threatened to have the windows broken if his wishes were not immediately obeyed. He passed a stout stick to a member of the jury to be used to smash the windows if he was not obeyed.

The man who could open all the windows was incredibly slow, so Mr Justice Maule wasted no time in ordering all the windows to be smashed. *The Times* reported on what happened:

> The smashing of the glass, as it came tumbling on the heads of the people below, and
> peals of laughter which were in consequence elicited from the bar and the whole

court, produced a scene which will be remembered by those who witnessed the occurrence. His Lordship, evidently wincing under the ridicule which his eccentric behaviour had excited, intimated, in not the most calm and dignified manner, and at the same time looking down upon the bar, that those gentlemen who wished to indulge in such indecorous behaviour had better go and indulge themselves out of the court …

At length, the court resumed its normal business and there was no problem with the hot air.

In 1821 there had been a riot at Stamford and a certain Mr Williams was indicted for breaking windows at the home of a Mr Hunt. Although the defence lawyer argued that there had been no riot, the judge disagreed, saying that no man on his oath could say that the vents had not been a riot. The jury withdrew and after two hours, eleven of the jury could agree but one man held out. Might the eleven men be discharged? The judge said that was impossible.

The jury then spent another five hours and there was no change. The resolute juryman told the court that he could not 'reconcile it to his conscience' that Mr Williams had riotously demolished the said windows. The judge would not let him withdraw. The man said, 'I would sooner eat mortar from the ceiling than give in.' With that state of affairs, the jury would have had to go with the judge to Nottingham, so they thought long and hard and finally handed in a note to the judge at the lodgings by the castle saying that they agreed for the defendant. No mortar had to be eaten that night.

⁍ KNIGHTS TEMPLARS ⁍

Our modern image of the chivalric medieval knight is that of the white surcoat and red cross: it could be Ivanhoe or Lionheart, but in reality this image describes a warrior of the Knights Templar order, founded in 1120 when King Baldwin of Jerusalem let the new brotherhood have his palace, in what had once been Aqsa Mosque. For that reason they became known as Templars, as their base was a famous temple. They had been formed in order to protect pilgrims travelling to and from the Holy Land after the First Crusade of 1095, but their remit soon extended to a number of other duties and responsibilities.

The Templars sometimes produced pictures of themselves, so we know what they would have looked like on campaign. A fresco on the wall of the Templar's church at San Bevignate in Italy shows a knight with a broad hat, bearded, and with a shield bearing the arms of the Templars. A more famous drawing, used in Matthew Paris' chronicles of the abbey of St Albans, shows two knights riding one horse, visors down and shields raised at the side.

The established images of the Templars hint at only one side of their incredibly versatile lifestyles and careers as 'soldiers militant' for God.

The order was to last for over 200 years, until Pope Clement IV in 1312 issued a papal bull removing their property, and then in 1314 two of the leaders, James of Molay and Geoffrey of Charnay, were cruelly burned at the stake in Paris.

The Knights Templar, though they began as warriors against bandits, eventually became landowners and farmers, and they established a network of centres called preceptories. The land around Lincoln contained two notable ones, at Eagle and at Temple Bruer. After the Domesday Book of 1086, there were seven settlements in Lincolnshire as a whole. There was usually a Knight in control of each preceptory, and at Eagle this figure would be in control of the Lincoln settlements.

A specimen of the Domesday book.

The Knights were notable for their ability to reclaim poor land and make it workable farmland.

One reason for the Knights' success in Lincolnshire was their benefactor, Roger Mowbray, who had land at Axholme. He had been a crusader, and had fought in a battle at the tender age of eighteen. He took part in the Battle of Lincoln, fighting for King Stephen, and lost much of his land. But he still had land to give, even after his exploits fighting the enemy in the Holy Land, and he gave the Templars land and woods at Keadby and services of tenant at Beltoft. The Knights clearly saw the woodland and wasteland as a challenge; they won fertile land from what was seen as useless common.

At Temple Bruer, however, it was ideal land for grazing. It was sited at a crossroads between Lincoln and Sleaford, and it became a successful place for them, having around 400 sheep and 100 pigs in 1246. The agents of the king actually bought sacks of wool from the Knights in 1298. The settlement extended quite a distance, with no fewer than 1185 tenants.

Temple Bruer was remarked upon by travellers and artists through the centuries, long after its decline. The traveller John Leland wrote of it in Tudor times, saying that, 'There be greate old vast buildings but rude at this place.' He also noticed the circular temple, and this was the design of all Templar buildings made after the original Church of the Holy Sepulchre in Jerusalem. Temple Bruer was later painted by Thomas Hearn and by Samuel Buck. When it was excavated, the first digger, Dr Oliver, tended to succumb to the bizarre myths and fantasies about the order

Temple Bruer Tower. (Photograph by
Robin Jones)

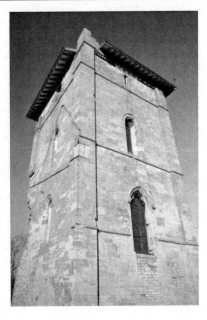

and only when St John Hope, in
1908, worked on the site did we
have a detailed and more realistic
appraisal.

Although relations between the
Templars and the locality were
generally good, there was trouble
in 1308 and the gatehouses and
small towers did not repel the
forces of the law at this time, as four
brother Knights were taken and
arrested. Even their chaplain, John
of Evesham, was taken away. They
were powerful, and in local power
games sometimes the law was used
in those days to help give one force the edge over another.

Eagle, on the other hand, was a notable Templar hospital, given a grant
from King Stephen and then expanded in the time of Henry II. There
was a higher proportion of older Knights and brothers at Eagle than any
other place in Britain. It was a fully subsistent community, with a barn,
hall, chapel and mill. The daily life of the Templar brothers was disciplined
and rigorous. The work on the farm or other physical labour at Eagle
would have been done in between services, starting with Prime Mass at
six in the morning, Terce prayers at nine, Sext Mass at noon, Nones and
Vespers through to dusk. The last prayers of the day would have been at
Compline. But they were military men too, and there would be time
allotted to cleaning and checking armour and weapons.

Everything in the average day was orderly and hierarchical. When they
sat down to eat, Knights would take the first sitting, then sergeants, then
the rest. Clerks would read texts to the Knights as they ate. These things
were all set out in the Statutes of the order.

The end of the Knights' Templar was savage and severe. We have to
imagine a massive operation across Europe, in which the forces of the
establishment moved against the preceptories and took men away,
throwing them into prison. In France, as early as 1307, the Templars in
the land had been arrested on the orders of King Philip IV. At Eagle, eight
Templars were arrested, including the Preceptor, Simon Stretche and four

of the men died in Lincoln Castle. There were elderly men among them, such as John de Waddon, a priest who had served the Templars for twenty years, and Henry de la Wold, who had put in thirty years of service. They were all tried in the early months of 1310; of the eleven who were actually interrogated, it was Henry de la Wold who described how he had been kissed on the mouth by the Templar Master when he had formally joined the order. This statement was ill-advised.

This was all because of the rule book of the order and the drive to distort and misinterpret this ritual by the powers in the land at the time. The nature of the absolution given by the Master was one of the main points of vulnerability when they came under attack. Whatever else went on at Lincoln, it eventually led to the Lincoln Templars being taken to London a year after the first interrogations.

The imprint of the Templars in and around Lincoln was significant. The personnel of the order around the city in 1338, for instance, included a Preceptor, a Squire, two chaplains and a clerk. The Knights also owned property in Lincoln itself, including the house they leased to Aaron the Jew for 3s a year. In the county as a whole, it has been estimated that they owned 11,460 acres in 1185. A mighty force with a massive economic structure fell in the violent years of the early fourteenth century, and Lincoln felt that collapse as much as any place

Later, the Hospitallers took over much of the estates and now, a visitor to Lincolnshire will see plenty of evidence of their involvement in the landscape, from Christs Hospitaller street at the top of Steep Hill, to the range of remains strung along the A15 road between Spital in the Street and Lincoln.

⚜ LIBEL AND ADVENTURE ⚜

The story began simply enough: in May 1937 the fishing boat from Grimsby, *The Girl Pat*, arrived home in Portsmouth harbour after a long and adventurous journey around the world. The trip had become so famous that the ship was to be put on display at Portsmouth in order to raise money for charity. But that was merely the quiet conclusion to the first part of the tale. After that, matters led to the High Court of Justice.

Commander Lawrence said that *The Girl Pat* had taken him to the Azores and that he had 'never been to sea in a better boat'. However, rather different reports about the boat began to circulate in the area, eventually leading to the publication of a best-selling book – and to a high-profile libel trial. Before that triumphant return, it seems that the ship had been stolen by her captain, Orsborne, and he and his crew set off on a long adventure in her. When Orsborne and his men were tracked down and arrested, they had what the newspapers at the time said was 'the effrontery to say that they were told to scuttle the ship and that rather than that, they ran away with her.' The skipper was arrested and brought back to England for trial. The Central Criminal Court stepped in and demanded a police enquiry following that allegation. Orsborne was sent to prison, of course, along with his brother. In order to back up their extraordinary allegation they said that the ship was damaged before they left, that she was not properly equipped for fishing, and that there was no food stored on board. Clearly, Orsborne's statement implied that a major fishing company, Marstrand's of Auckland Road Fish Docks in Grimsby, were guilty of a criminal action.

Unfortunately for *The Daily Herald*, they had reported the statement, as had the publishers of a book about the case, Hutchinson and Co. Their book, *The Voyage of 'The Girl Pat'* by Skipper Orsborne, had sold very well. The printers, The Anchor Press, were also involved. At the heart of the concept of libel is that there has been 'the publication of false, defamatory

Sunset at Portsmouth Harbour. (Photograph by Editor5807)

words' and that the plaintiff must show that 'the statement made was defamatory and was made in the third person'. The skipper had said that his employers had told him to get rid of the trawler, which had resulted in newspaper reports and a book. Unfortunately for the two publishers, this statement turned out to be untrue.

Marstrand had the famous Sir Patrick Hastings representing them, so they looked very likely to win damages – as indeed they did. Hastings further suggested that the book had been written by a journalist, as he felt that the captain would not capable of producing such writing. Therefore, it must be a work of fiction. But there was no laughing matter when it came to the words provided by the publishers: 'Daredevil Dad Orsborne took the vessel out of Grimsby on an ostensible fishing trip only to decide when she had gained open sea to change her course and run her anywhere.'

Then the facts were given, rather than the fantasy. *The Times* reported:

> The truth about *The Girl Pat* was that she was a trawler of about 25 tons, which was used for net fishing in shallow water. She was a new ship and had only just been

overhauled when she was taken out by Orsborne. She had twelve days' supplies on board, there was a chart, the winch was in perfect order, and she was fully equipped.

The rogue involved in those spurious memoirs had said that all those provisions were not available on board. When the managing director of Marstrands was asked by Hastings what the effect on his company the allegations would have, he replied: 'If I were a fisherman I would not enter employment with such a firm.' But the plaintiffs had gathered all necessary evidence, even to the extent of producing a Danish seaman with a Master's certificate who testified that the winch on the ship had been fine when he tested it. However, the public were still unconvinced, and things went from bad to worse for Marstrands' employees, whose sufferings included 'unpleasant social experiences.' Clearly, there had been bad feeling – and also a twisted and cruel sense of humour – around Grimsby when the story broke.

Another action was taken, this time against other papers. Journalists loved the idea that the ship might be undermanned and that there had been a directive to scuttle her. Some writers made high drama of it all, and one writer even quoted some lines from Rudyard Kipling's poem, *The Ballad of the Bolivar* (1890) in which these lines appear: 'Overloaded, undermanned, meant to founder, we/Euchred God Almighty's storm, bluffed the eternal sea!' There was no denying what that implied, amplifying the astounding accusations made by Orsborne.

The long fiasco ended with an abject apology from Valentine Holmes of the press. He said that he desired, on behalf of the defendants, publicly to express their deep regret for circulating the skipper's story. The Grimsby firm of solicitors, Deacon and Co., must have had some strange tales to tell when they went back north, as there had been almost as much drama in the High Court as there had been out at sea.

❧ LITTLE SAINT HUGH ❧

A Lincoln man called John de Lexington has a lot to answer for. In 1255, when he was in a crowd of people who had found the bloated body of a child in a well, he started putting around a story that there was a terrible Jewish custom of indulging in an annual murder of a Gentile child. The body found in the well was that of little Hugh, son of Beatrice, who had been searching the city high and low just a month before, after her son failed to return from playing out in the streets.

Jew's House in Lincoln.

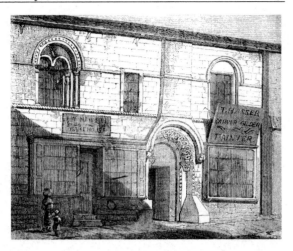

The mystery at the heart of this story is that Hugh did die and was found in a cess pool by a group of Jews when they gathered in the home of a man called Jopin to celebrate a marriage. The experience the crowd had is almost too horrendous to contemplate: being together for a happy occasion and then discovering the drowned body of a small boy in their midst. But things turned out badly for the Jewish community of the city: Jopin, as a result of Lexington's ridiculous urban myth, was tortured to the point at which he confessed to the killing – obviously speaking under extreme duress. But the offer of sparing his life if he confessed was on the table in the rather extreme negotiations.

Now we enter the barbarous world of medieval anti-semitism: Henry III was in need of money and he had foolishly arranged for income from Jewish communities to pass out of his hands. Being an absolute monarch, he could create laws when needed, and it seemed to him a perfect moment to exploit the disgraced Jews of Lincoln's community. He arranged to tax Jewish groups who had been

Henry III.

Newport Gate, Lincoln, where the well once stood, as it appeared two centuries ago.

guilty of a crime, and so poor Jopin was to suffer. He was hanged after being publicly humiliated and a group of other Jews were sent to London for trial. As for little Hugh – he became a saint and a martyr. He was only a commoner, but named after Saint Hugh, Bishop of Lincoln. What happened around this time in the city was only one chapter in a whole series of terrible persecutions against Jews in England.

In 1189, when the build-up to what was to be the Third Crusade was taking place, there was a rumour that Richard the Lionheart had called for the killing of all the Jews in his kingdom, and mobs were out in the streets. There was also the despicable mass murder of Jews in York, only half a century before the events in Lincoln. Here, the Jewish population of York had gathered in Clifford's Tower near the castle, for safety from attack. Sadly, they all killed themselves rather than being taken by the wild mobs in the streets.

In Lincoln, in the Dernstall (the Jewish quarter), there had already been a certain degree of discrimination, well before the furore over the supposed murder of Hugh. This was in the early years of the thirteenth century, when a decree issued by the Council of the Church had effected open separatism, by calling the Jews blasphemers and making them dress differently from Christians, and by preventing them furthering their careers by mixing in Gentile society. The paradox at the centre of commercial life in this context – that the local economy needed credit but that usury was sinful – provided just the kind of moral complication that turns men's wits and opens up events to wild prejudice.

As for little Hugh, one advantage was that more people would come to Lincoln to visit his shrine, and that could only be good for trade. But above these practical developments, a myth was engendered about the supposed murder, and this was sustained in literature. A poem of 1783 called 'The ballad of Little Sir Hugh' has the lines:

> She's led him in through ae dark door,
> and sae has she thro nine;
> she's laid him on a dressing table
> and stick it him like a swine …

As time went on, the story was embellished; one account even claims that when the child's body was eventually found by the Christians, 'the hands and feet were pierced with wounds' as if the boy had indeed been crucified. Even Chaucer mentions the event in *The Canterbury Tales*, where he has these lines:

Aaron the Jew's house today. (Photograph by Richard Croft)

O yonge Hew of Lincoln, slain also

with cursed Jewes, as it is notable,

for it is but a little while ago.

A writer much nearer the actual time, Matthew Paris, recounts the events as if it were a matter of fact:

the Jews of Lincoln stole a boy of eight years of age, whose name was Hugh, and having shut him up in a room quite out of the way… they sent to all the cities of England where Jews lived, and summoned some of their sect who lived in the city to be present at a sacrifice.

The fate of the other ninety-two Jews was that they were taken to London and tried; Paris reports that 'on St Clement's Day eighteen of the richer and higher order of the Jews of the city of Lincoln were dragged to new gibbets and were hung up, an offering to the winds.'

What traces are left of this myth are few indeed. There are the remains of a tiny tomb on the north side of the choir aisle in the cathedral. In the eighteenth century a skeleton was actually found during an excavation, and it was in fact a body of a small child. In the Jew's Court house near the bottom of Steep Hill there is a well which is thought to be the well in question (though after its discovery by a Mr Harry Staples it was found to be only 3ft deep) from the first telling of the tale. The well there, it seems, had been constructed by a Mr Dodgson, much more recently than the time of Hugh. But there is another line of thought, and this traditionally relates that the famous well was where Newport Arch stands.

The Jewish quarter was from Dernstall Lock, at the southern end of the main street, to the southern fringe of Bailgate. The events concerning the taxation imposed on the community after the Hugh affair and the savagery brought about on the victim, Jopin, have to be placed in a context in which there had been very powerful Jewish citizens in Lincoln and not so long before the death of Hugh. Most notable there was Aaron, who lived in the northern uphill streets somewhere, though not in the house at the top of Steep hill now called 'Aaron's House' for tourists, opposite the Harlequin bookshop. Aaron was very rich and influential in his time (1166-1186) and the historian Mansell Sympson claims that he was 'possibly the most important financial agent in the kingdom'.

Aaron arranged loans for many powerful men, including the Archbishop of Canterbury and Earl of Leicester. It is not difficult to see that, given a crisis such as a trumped-up murder charge, the community as a whole could find easy scapegoats in the ranks of those to whom they owed money; this was the risk factor that all Jews lived with, like the Sword of Damocles, in their lives among Christian groups. Not long after these events, in 1290, the Jews in this land were expelled. The story of little Saint Hugh was just one of the influential events, spurred on by racism, along the way of that difficult journey of the people in exile, looking for understanding and tolerance.

The truth of the supposed murder will never be found; all we know is that, as the famous antiquary Bishop Thomas Percy said, the whole charge is surely 'groundless and malicious, such as been imputed to the Jews for 750 years or more.' The story is as fabricated as the boy's name: he was never canonised, so there is a dark irony in his 'sainthood' as the tale goes on. Even as late as the middle of the nineteenth century, as R. Brimley Johnson notes in an anthology of ballads, 'It was known to the labourers of Lincolnshire in very recent years'. In the poem in question the tale extends to a ghost story, with the spirit of Hugh singing:

Gae hame, gae hame, my mither dear:
Prepare my winding sheet;
And at the back of merry Lincoln
The morn I will you meet.'

⁕ LONG DROP MAN ⁕

There was a jest going around England in mid-Victorian times, and it concerned a shoemaker who lived in the small Lincolnshire village of Horncastle:

If pa killed ma, who would kill pa?
Marwood.

This referred to William Marwood, shoemaker, but also public executioner for Britain. This was a responsibility he was proud to carry out and his professional attitude to this most macabre job gave him wide notoriety in his time.

When Marwood was starting to take an interest in the subject of execution, the hangman with most national responsibility was William Calcraft – and he had a bad reputation. He was fond of a drink and was not always able to help a villain swiftly to the next world. For centuries, the business of hanging had been carried out with no real thought given to the humane exit of the criminal. It would normally take a while for the individual to die, hence the expression 'hangers-on' (the friends of a man being executed would hang on his legs to hasten the death).

Marwood began experimenting with using the weight of the criminal and adjusting the length of rope and the nature of the drop itself. He practised in a way that worked out the quick snapping of the vertebrae, rather than the usual method of asphyxiation. In an interview given in 1879 he stated, 'My system is humane... my object is to spare suffering. The old plan was to kill by strangling; mine is by dislocation.' It is hard to fathom why a man following a trade in a rural community would take an interest in such things, but he did and the more he read accounts of hangings, the more his self-belief grew. He started writing letters, attempting to argue his case in the right places. It is very difficult to see this quiet man, a craftsman born in Goulceby in 1818, developing such interests. His background was against any such notorious work; his father was an illiterate shoemaker, with ten children. It seems likely that William himself was not outstanding as a wordsmith, but he had basic literacy as he was able to write letters, many of which have been preserved.

By 1872, he carried out his first execution: this was on Francis Horry, a man who had killed his wife. Marwood's humane method had given the man a quick death; the shoemaker had a new career. According to recent research and publication, Marwood carried out executions of 167 men and nine women. This is far above his own claim, that he had done almost 400.

Marwood had a flair for what we would now call 'spin'. He had a card made, stating that he was an executioner, giving his address. People would buy shoe laces from him and be happy to pay more than usual for the celebrity angle. Marwood enjoyed this; he made his workshop at 6 Church lane, Horncastle, something of an attraction. When he wrote to prospective employers in his new trade, he sent some cards. Descriptions of him talk about his eyes, which were 'quiet, resolute and penetrating'. The interviewer who met him in 1897 said that Marwood's hands were 'knotted, twisted, vigorous hands, the hands of a man who had worked with them for years at some severe manual labour and who could use them with Herculean strength and tenacity if required.'

There is a story of Marwood meeting a man on a train, who asked whether they had met before. Marwood's reply was, 'It couldn't have been at eight o'clock in the morning.' He travelled extensively in his role

William Marwood's bust in
Madame Tussauds.

William Calcraft.

as executioner and was very well organised. In one letter, written to his wife, he gives a clear idea of a typical schedule; he had come back from Clonmel in Ireland and now:

> … arrived at about three o'clock this morning for Birmingham, arrived about eleven o'clock today. I am now in Birmingham with the Governor waiting to see the Governor at Bristol at half past two today, then I leave for Cambridge… if all well I shall return on Monday night or Tuesday morning. I hope all is well at home. Tell my poor boy Nero [his dog] that his master is coming home.

On his travels, he earned well; for a job in Galway the sheriff wrote to him, confirming that the charge would be £20 for the day. He attracted such attention that people wrote to him, asking to be his assistant. Overall, he was very high-profile, and some of his clients are notorious names in the history of crime in Britain.

M

⚜ MADAME MIARD ⚜

In 1843, the Reverend Herbert Marsh of Barnack found himself requesting an investigation into the identity and past of a woman who had arrived in the area, claiming that she had had an immoral liaison with him in France some years before. The woman said that she was Madame Miard and she worked hard to speak to the clergyman's family, before turning up at church to spread gossip. In time she also set up house in Stamford, so that she could easily cause annoyance in the area.

Madame Miard delighted in shadowing her victim, even as far as a church in Peterborough. She told stories of herself and Herbert having a torrid affair in Paris and London and it was all becoming too much for the good vicar. He went to the law. Investigations began and the mysterious woman was found to be someone called Durhais, a known confidence trickster and impostor. The police knew her as a lady who usually travelled with an older female companion, whom she usually described as her aunt. Together they would raise mayhem and harass victims, mainly for the sheer thrill of it.

Miard and aunt were seen as a conspiratorial duo in the eyes of the law and they were destined for Lincoln assizes, where punishment was meted out. The vicar slept easily after that, we suppose – unless of course he did have secrets in his past and was singled out for a valid reason.

⚜ MAGISTRATES PAY UP ⚜

The late Victorian years and the Edwardian period saw a rapid increase in beer shops. Workers often had a drink in the early morning on the way to work, and then stopped off again for a beer, or more, on the way home. Ann Robinson was trading at that time, with hot competition down the road in the form of Temperance magistrates who were trying to use the law to shut her down. As a widow, she would have been alone in her fight.

But luckily, she had very talented solicitors. She was sure that the magistrates were being most unfair and took them to court. In the Market Rasen petty sessions in October 1893, she appealed against a sentence she had been given for one such case, on the basis that insufficient proof had been tendered before the Bench, and that the White Lion Inn was not at all badly conducted, as had been claimed. Ann was feeling victimised. Amazingly, she was successful, and the justices were ordered to pay £29 14s and 10p 'for the seasonable charges and costs of the said appellant by them sustained and incurred'.

What Ann had done was to enlist the help of the brewery in Lincoln with whom she worked. Their man, and the local solicitor, had chased up every charge and reference, even sending a man to check on the stated offences. But there was also an issue of a larger scale. Questions had been asked in Parliament in July that year: the Home Secretary was asked if a Temperance advocate was allowed to sit as a magistrate, and he had answered in the affirmative. Obviously, there were likely to be Temperance men on the Benches up and down the land. The Temperance Movement was gaining strength as the beer shops increased and marches through the towns, in which Temperance banners were held high, were common sights. Taking the pledge was fashionable, although in many cases it was a matter of show rather than resolve.

In 1904, the Licensing Act tackled the question of the proliferation of licensed premises and reduced their number to a considerable extent. There had been statutory licensing of alehouses by justices in England since 1552 and the annual Brewster Sessions had become an institution, dealing with a motley assemblage of licensing cases. The beer shops had arrived after 1830, when the Beer Act was passed – but Ann's place was an inn. What had affected her was the 1872 act, which dealt more directly with drunkenness – hence her conviction, which was for 'selling to a drunkard'. We can appreciate the scale of the problem of social drinking when we note that in 1869, according to Paul Jennings, there were 118,500 licences given for premises to sell alcoholic drinks. There was a gradual decline after the 1872 Act and by 1901 there were 'a little under 103,000 licences'.

That national picture places Ann Robinson's fight to remain in business in context: she stood against the tide of repression and reform because she felt that she was the victim of an injustice. The statement resulting from her appeal reads that 'the refusal to renew such licence was contrary to law and inequitable', and so Revd William Waldo Cooper, Louis Charles Tennyson d'Eyncourt, Cook Holdershaw and Gerard Young esquires would have had to reach into their considerable pockets and pay up. The member of the Tennyson family, Louis Charles, had been a Metropolitan

Police magistrate also; he died in 1896. As for Ann, she returned to her work with, undoubtedly, a wonderful feeling of triumph, although we can be sure that she spent some time in the tap room and was more severe with the noisy drunks.

She had been one unusual instance in a national debate. The Bishop of Chester spoke out on the 'drink question' and caused a stir. One correspondent wrote to *The Times* to insist that the much-maligned landlords were actually worthy of a second look, writing that, 'The reports presented by the police to the licensing magistrates at the Brewster Sessions now being held furnish pretty conclusive evidence that publicans are by no means what their enemies imagine them to be, but are essentially a law-abiding section of the community.'

⚜ MOLLY GRIME ⚜

The tale of Molly Grime is a charming Glentham legend, told suitably by a correspondent of Ethel Rudkin for her book on Lincolnshire folklore:

> If you want to get to Newell's Well you go from Caenby four cross-roads straight down Glentham Road till you come to the bend, where a lane goes off to your left and there's a little bit of plantin'... And past that there's a way through... The well is close against you, a great square stone place it is with a great slab of stone on top; peep in and you can see the water bubblin' up in two or three places at once... It's beautiful water and on the hottest day it's as cold as cold.

The well was named after a man of that name. It was said that he left money for seven poor widows of the area and that every Good Friday the ladies had to take water from that spring and wash a stone coffin: that was the coffin with a figure on called Molly Grime. A man from Spital said to Ethel, 'Molly Grime they calls it... what I often wonders is, what's become of the money!' The story must have gained currency around the whole district because people are recorded to have said that a child with a dirty face will be called a Molly Grime. Also, the money from Newell was paid in earlier times because there was a recorded rent charge noted in the 1830s called 'Grimes'.

⚜ MR LOVELEY'S HOUSE ⚜

There has always been something about Branston that has attracted travellers and visitors to notice fine details, such as the rather cryptic note of Pevsner in 1964 that 'No one should miss Mr Loveley's gate piers at Branston', which actually refers to the amazing folly of Stonefield House. Pevsner, writing much later, explained the figures of monkeys on the piers: 'There'll be a good monkey in that house [meaning a mortgage],' says one. Says Mr Lovely, 'I'll show them where the monkeys will be.'

This is on the Sleaford Road and since 1985 has been classified by English Heritage as a Grade II listed building. Pevsner would have been delighted to know that the 'folly' was treasured. In fact, there is something about Branston that attracts both creative flair and workmanlike application. This combination has made it one of the most attractive and engaging communities around the city of Lincoln, with its own special qualities and its biographies of lords, clergymen and minor celebrities. Most Lincolnshire people go there to chill out, treat themselves, get married or just relish the sense of history. A closer look at its rootedness in a fascinating past surely invites us to look closer and discover things beyond the church and the Hall, however enthralling these places are.

Branston Hall. (Photograph by Matthew Smith)

n

⁂ NODDER, THE PRISON GHOST ⁂

This is the story of a lorry-driver lodger from Hell, who committed the most depraved and wicked of crimes.

Frederick Nodder moved into new lodgings in Newark in 1935, where his landlady was Mrs Tinsley. He didn't stay long, but he made a mark with the children. To them he was 'Uncle Fred.' He was clearly a man who was difficult to live with, at least in the adult world. When he moved on to East Retford, he still proved to be a handful for the landlady, with his bad habits and tendency to create a mess. Nodder appears to be a man with a mission – to destroy everything and everyone around who could be considered weak or vulnerable.

But back in Newark, the large family of Tinsleys was now one short of the usual number. Little Mona, aged ten, was missing after not returning home from her school on 5 January 1937. Her father, Wilfred, was frantic with worry and went to search the school for his little girl. Mona's poor father was distraught with anxiety and after the police were called, the description went out: she was wearing a knitted suit and wore Wellingtons. But a boy called Willie Placket recalled seeing Mona talking to a man and said that he would recognise the man if he saw him again. A Mrs Hird had also seen Mona with a man who 'was a lodger with the girl's mother'. The net was closing in on the person described as 'a man with staring eyes'.

Nodder had a hook nose and his moustache was ginger. He seems to have been memorable, as lots of people remembered him on that journey with little Mona. A bus conductor recalled him. The police traced him to Retford and he was picked up. He had been living as Hudson, and was the father of a child living locally.

Mona had been seen with 'Uncle Fred' and consequently, as Mona was now officially missing and the anxiety increased, Nodder was interviewed. His story was that he had given the girl a lift to Sheffield and then put Mona on a bus to her aunt's in Worksop. It was all highly suspicious and

'Nodder.' (Drawing by Laura Carter)

he was arrested for abduction. There was no body, so there was no murder charge. In court, the abduction still stood and he was sent to prison.

As he was in custody and there was a feeling that Mona had been attacked or even killed, a massive search began; 1,000 people joined in to search areas between Retford and Newark. It was such a wide stretch of land that the police from Nottinghamshire, Lincolnshire and Derbyshire all spent time and manpower on the case. Scotland Yard now sent men to step up the campaign: the Chesterfield canal was dragged. Nodder had been tried at Birmingham, but now off he went to Nottingham to face a murder charge.

So began Fred Nodder's period inside the walls of Lincoln prison. Only three months after his trial, Mona's body was found in the river Idle close to Bawtry. She had been strangled. Nodder was in court again, trying to tell tales to escape the noose, but nothing he could say did him any good. The presiding judge, Mr Justice Macnaughton, said, 'Justice has slowly, but surely, overtaken you and it only remains for me to pronounce the sentence which the law and justice require…'

Norman Birkett had spoken for the prosecution; it was to be his last trial appearing for the Crown. It was a terrible case, with a widespread sense of outrage around it, as Nodder had sexually assaulted Mona before killing her. 'Uncle Fred' had turned out to be a monster. The photos of him show a man with a matching flat cap and scarf of small check pattern and a thick overcoat. His eyes are piercing and he shows a face to the world that expresses nothing substantial: 'something is missing in him' is a comment that is often said of these types of killers. Ironically, this man who had created so much pain and torment to others lived in a place called Peacehaven.

He was sentenced to hang. A few days after Christmas 1937, he was in the hands of the hangman and left this world. Or did he? He was hanged in Lincoln Prison on Greetwell Road, and his last moments would have been on the wing of the execution suite. He would have fallen through the trap to dangle and die – very quickly – taking less time to perish than his victim had done. The corpse was taken down and buried, with quicklime, as was the custom. But was that the last of Fred Nodder inside the prison walls? Some think not.

Since then, there has been development in the prison, as there has with almost every other Victorian building. Staff report sightings of a man walking the corridors, with a dark overcoat and flat check cap. One report describes turning a corner to see a man with piercing eyes coming towards him. Some have merely glimpsed the profile, with the hooked nose and moustache.

There are many dark roads and corners around Greetwell Road. A spirit could wander those streets, a restless, evil entity like 'Uncle Fred'. If the tales are true, then this evil man is as restless now as he was in life – always open to do some horrible mischief. In fairly recent times, when building work was done on the prison site, the graves of executed prisoners were taken up and carried to the city cemetery. The more serious ghost-hunters date the appearances of the ghost of 'Uncle Fred' to that time. When the ground opened up, his nasty spirit walked into the world again to disturb the unwary. The man with the staring eyes, if he exists in spirit form, will still try his hardest to unsettle the unsuspecting night-walker. Nodder was always a man who haunted, loitered, and watched people.

Even if the Lincoln walker, striding through Greetwell Road, has no belief in ghosts, a glance at the forbidding high and dark walls of the prison there will do enough to suggest that this killer had no pleasant stay in his last hours on earth.

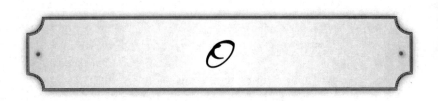

✥ OLD JEFFREY ✥

In John Wesley's short memoir of the hauntings at Epworth rectory, written in 1784, he ends with his father's response to a call from friends that he should leave his home: 'No, let the Devil flee from me: I will never flee from the Devil!' Soon after, the paranormal activities ceased.

To visit the rectory now is to experience peace and withdrawal from the troubles of the world. A tour around the rooms, even the attic where a certain spirit called Old Jeffrey was supposedly active, is to feel relaxed and somehow taken back to quieter times. The place is just off the Gainsborough road, south of Epworth, an easy walk from the market square of the town, and you walk past the memorial statue of John Wesley as you do so.

In the years around 1716-1719, there is enough evidence to suggest that the rectory certainly had a noisy and frightening poltergeist. John's account, based on questioning of family and servants in the year 1720, relates tales of knockings, objects being moved and even of the family mastiff dog being so scared that it cowered and ran for cover by the side of John's parents.

The large family gradually began to be familiar with the process of the hauntings. John relates that his sisters became attuned to the knocks and sounds. After hearing knocks on their bed-head, they would say

The famous John Wesley.

Wesley's signature in *Appletons'*
Cyclopedia of American
Biography, 1900.

that Jeffrey was coming and that it was time to go to sleep. But it was no joke – experiencing this sound in those tiny, ill-lit rooms and corridors, and feeling that there could be an emanation at any time, in any one of the many rooms, was a terrifying reality. For instance, nothing had happened in John's father's study until one night when he went into his room and the door slammed open so violently that it shook him and almost knocked him to the floor.

Mr Wesley repeatedly tried to address the poltergeist, sometimes feeling that it was the spirit of his dead son, Samuel, and at other times being sure that it was a malevolent sprite. On one occasion he said to the spirit, 'Thou deaf and dumb Devil, why dost thou fright these children, that cannot answer thee themselves?' In response came a familiar knocking and then some hours of peace from its torments.

Trouble seems to have started in 1716 when a servant, Robert Brown, was sitting resting in the late evening. He and a maid heard knocking at the door, but when it was opened there was nobody to be seen. But when poor Robert went to his bed, he saw in front of him, in the garret, a handmill whirling in the air. The session of torture from the other world ended with the ghost making the sound of a turkey-cock by Robert's bedside.

There seems to have been a hex on the building. When the place was on fire in 1709, and people thought that everyone had been brought out to safety, the outline of a boy was spotted upstairs and he was brought out to safety. The boy was no less than John Wesley himself. So at least there is some small piece of good fortune in this troublesome tale of Epworth's rectory, which is now a tourist destination.

Old Jeffrey, as he came to be named, was called so by Emily, one of the Wesley daughters. She discovered that an old man had died there and that this restless soul was probably him. One of the most intriguing aspects of the haunting is the fact that activity was more marked when family prayers were occasionally not spoken; what that tells us remains a mystery, but the one certain fact is the attic where Jeffrey is supposed to have focused his nuisances and terror is still rather bare and unnaturally silent. You feel an atmosphere as you walk in, even today. Though a peaceful place, the rectory may still have some residual energies from Jeffrey and his nasty tricks.

To Mr. Samuel Wesley, from his Mother.

DEAR SAM,   January 12, 1716-7.

THIS evening we were agreeably surprised with your pacquet, which brought the welcome news of your being alive, after we had been in the greatest panic imaginable, almost a month, thinking either you was dead, or one of your brothers by some misfortune been killed.

The reason of our fears, is as follows. On the first of December, our maid heard, at the door of the dining-room, several dismal groans, like a person in extremes, at the point of death. We gave little heed to her relation, and endeavoured to laugh her out of her fears. Some nights (two or three) after, several of the family heard a strange knocking in divers places, usually three or four knocks at a time, and then stayed a little. This continued every night for a fortnight; sometimes it was in the gar-ret, but most commonly in the nursery, or green chamber.

A section of one of the letters from Samuel Wesley's mother describing the long-drawn out haunting at Epworth. They were reprinted in various collections at the end of the eighteenth century; this example is from *New Wonderful Magazine*.

A steady walk through Epworth, stopping off at the Red Lion, where John used to sit sometimes, then past the high walls by the side of the through road, gives the visitor no idea of the former restless ghost who roamed that area and who terrorised the Wesley family for so long. But in the end, Mr Wesley would not 'flee'.

𝒫

⚜ PHANTOM HIKERS ⚜

I am including here something from personal experience. It happened on the lonely B road from Kirton to Scunthorpe. One night in 1980, I travelled from Lincoln with two colleagues from work; it was snowing and stormy. The road was dark as we drove from Greetwell towards the junction at Mortal Ash Hill by Scunthorpe steelworks. My friends were deep in conversation and I was watching the woods at the side of the road. Suddenly, I saw the figure of a man struggling in the wind.

'Stop! There's an old man, he's in trouble,' I said. We all agreed that an old man should not be out in that weather. We pulled up and two of us went back to look for him, only 100 yards or so behind. There was absolutely no sign of the man. I have since heard that many people have seen the old man there, close to the junction with Holme Lane.

But to add to the mystery of this place, there is also another well-known hiker at almost exactly the same spot – this one a young woman. A correspondent tells me that this lady flags down drivers and asks for a lift to Kirton. Many have helped her and asked her to take a seat in the back of the car, only to find that, after the vehicle has started up and moved on for a short distance, the hiker has vanished.

⚜ POACHER TALES ⚜

Some years ago, a correspondent to *Lincolnshire Life* magazine addressed the subject of poachers. He had some staggering tales to tell, including reference to a man called John Fulton, who lived in Lincoln at the foot of Steep Hill. The writer recalled that Fulton 'had been bitten over every inch of his body by rats' and that one time when he met the poacher he was startled: 'I bought several good ferrets from him years ago and have seen him put a rat in one side of his shirt and a ferret in the other and let them fight around the back!'

Of course, Lincolnshire is forever linked with poachers, thanks to the song 'The Lincolnshire Poacher', in which the singer talks about his 'delight on a shiny night, in the season of the year.' The poachers were always meeting with the law, of course. The same writer to the magazine mentioned his fine of 5s in the Sessions House 'for carrying a gun without a licence' and having 'a folded 410 in the poacher's pocket' in his jacket. But sometimes the poachers' activities were far more serious, and back in the days of hanging a number of them ended their days on the gallows after killing gamekeepers.

In 1877, there was one of those common encounters between gamekeepers and poachers that often ended in nothing much, but at other times ended in murder or manslaughter. William Clarke and his friends were poaching pheasants at Eagle Wood in January of this year. There were four men, and they split into two pairs, Clarke going with a man called Garner to Norton Disney.

Henry Walker and his assistants were looking for poachers that night and they saw Clarke and Garner pass by. After being told to stop, Clarke decided to challenge the keepers and showed his gun, but they were pursued when they ran, and Clarke turned to shoot the pursuers. He shot Walker and the man died. Of course, the poachers were known; they had been seen. They were rounded up, except for Clarke, who had run away from the area. This then became a work for the detectives and the man for the job was Superintendent Brown of Kesteven, who doggedly followed his man until he finally had him cornered in Lowestoft. With the help of back-up, the killer was arrested – just a short period before he was due to sail for the continent.

All the poachers were on trial in Lincoln on 7 March, and there Garner identified Clarke as the killer. Marwood had another job, as Clarke was hanged and the others acquitted.

❧ QUAKES ❧

In the hours between 1.30 and 2 a.m. on Easter Sunday, 23 April 1905, Lincolnshire people experienced the horror of an earthquake. People in Lincoln and Gainsborough were roused from sleep and the police were out on patrol in case they were needed. The worst of it was felt in Yorkshire and also in Nottinghamshire. That year there were quakes across Europe: France, Lyons, Chamonix and the Rhone were hit, and then also in Italy at Turin and Domodossola.

Yet that was not the first to hit Lincoln. In 1185 the cathedral was struck by a powerful quake. The epicentre was perhaps in the North Sea or the Dogger Bank. The cathedral was destroyed in that high intensity shock, as described in Holinshed's great chronicle of the Tudor years:

> … chanced a sore earthquake through all the parts of this land, such a one as the like had not been heard of in England, since the beginning of the world; for stones that lay couched fast in the earth were removed out of their places, houses were overthrown, and the great church of Lincoln rent from the top downwards …

❧ QUEEN ELEANOR'S HEART ❧

Eleanor of Castile, born in 1241, was the first queen consort of Edward I and she was also Countess of Pontieu, dying in 1290. In fact, it is in her death that she gives us a Lincolnshire tale of considerable interest. It seems that Edward and Eleanor really were a loving couple, with plenty of fun and laughter in their life together.

She was not simply a figurehead though; she was a patron of the Dominican order of friars, and she helped to found a number of priories. Eleanor was evidently an intellectual and also a very astute person when it came to politics, but her story comes home to life in Lincoln in the

Eleanor of Castille.

Edward I, also known as
'Longshanks' for his unusual
height, and as 'the hammer of
the Scots'.

The Great Seal of Edward I.

autumn of 1290. Then, Edward was holding a parliament at Clipstone in Nottinghamshire and Eleanor was travelling to be with him. However, she was ill and so she stayed with Richard de Weston near Harby.

Her condition deteriorated there and she received the last rites of the church, dying on the 28 November, aged forty-nine. Edward managed to get to her just before she passed away. Because Edward took her body to Westminster, he decided to place crosses at points on that journey – a notion borrowed from a similar action taken by the King of France, Louis IX. These 'Eleanor crosses' are in place from Lincoln to Charing Cross – the latter being in Whitehall, not at the Charing Cross we have today. One of the crosses was placed on St Peter's Hill and Grantham and that was later destroyed by Oliver Cromwell.

Her funeral took place at Westminster Abbey and her own tomb was made later, of marble with elaborate carvings. At Lincoln we have images of the couple in the cathedral. Contemplating the sad loss at Harby is inevitable on looking at the memorial. Edward memorably said, 'Living, I loved her dearly and I shall never cease to love her in death.' Her body was taken to St Catherine's Priory in Lincoln, where she was embalmed. Her heart was taken to Blackfriars' priory in London, as she had wished, but her other organs were interred at Lincoln.

⚘ RASEN BAD GUYS ⚘

Brothers Isaac and Thomas spent their lives moving between Lincoln and London, after Isaac had started his working life as a post boy in Lincoln when he was just twelve. Later, the young man was in the debtor's prison, put there by a Mr Rands. The resulting hatred from that imprisonment was to be the beginning of a path to infamy – so much so that the brothers provide one of the few Lincolnshire stories that made it into the famous *Newgate Calendar* of crime stories. After failing in business in London, the brothers crossed the line into criminality and began to earn a living as highway robbers.

The brothers covered a very large area in their crime: most parts of the east of England, from Epping to Lincolnshire felt their mark, robbing

The two Rasen brothers pictured committing another depredation upon the highway.

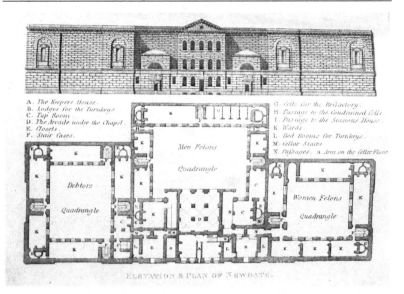

A. The Keepers House.
B. Lodges for the Turnkeys.
C. Tap Room.
D. The Arcade under the Chapel.
E. Closets.
F. Stair Cases.

G. Cells for the Refractory.
H. Passage to the Condemned Cells.
I. Passage to the Sessions House.
K. Wards.
L. Bed Rooms for Turnkeys.
M. Cellar Stairs.
N. Passages, a Area on the Cellar Floor.

Men Felons
Quadrangle

Debtors
Quadrangle

Women Felons
Quadrangle

ELEVATION & PLAN OF NEWGATE.

Taken from William Jackson's *Newgate Calendar,* this plan shows the elevation and internal layout of Newgate. The section marked with an H (in the upper left corner of the 'men felons' quadrangle'), shows the passage to the condemned cells.

on foot and on horseback in various places. But in January 1733 they were in Lincolnshire and at Dunholme, just a few miles north of Lincoln, they joined a man called William Wright. They all had a few drinks and then left for Market Rasen, going through Faldingworth. It was a perfect opportunity for the Hallams to make some easy money. They simply had to rob this man, as he was in his cups. At first they failed and he took off, but later, at Ings Gate, they met him again and killed him, cutting his throat to end his life. They wrapped the body in a cloth and then at Holton Beckering they drank again, and soon came across a post boy, a certain Thomas Gardiner. At this time, the mail was taken across the land between relay-points, and the carts were supposed to move at six miles an hour. Of course, these post boys, who were not armed, were easy prey for highwaymen; often it was argued that they were in league with robbers, as it was such a tempting and profitable crime.

In this case, it was well before some reforms that were made (in 1794) and young Thomas, just nineteen years of age, had his throat cut, and never reached his destination, Langworth. The Hallams waited for the post master, who they thought would also come along, but he did not. They went off with 25s and some food. They returned south and went to work around London again, but the news was out and a handsome reward advertised. They were arrested and taken to Lincoln.

Outside the city of Lincoln, the local post boys gathered to blow their horns as the killers were brought to gaol. Then in March, at the Lent assizes, the Hallams were tried before Mr Justice Probyn, who had just before this sat at the infamous Princess Serafina trial in London, at which the crime of sodomy was much publicised. Probyn was in no mood to consider anything that smacked of compassion and the two brothers were sentenced to be hanged. Isaac was hanged at Nettleham just north of Lincoln, and his body gibbeted at the scene, as was the custom then. His brother was hanged at Faldingworth. As N.V. Gagen has pointed out, the dates of the hangings are uncertain. The *Newgate Calendar* states that they were hanged on the 20 February, but other contemporary reports say 23 March and also 22 March. Whatever the exact date, justice was done and the post boys had a sense of revenge. The memorial in Nettleham preserves the memory of their barbarity and the severe justice done.

It is ironical that such rogues, typical of so many in their day, should have the questionable status of being a *Newgate Calendar* story, as there was nothing extraordinary about them; it was simply that they had been busy in London in their criminal activities, as well as in Lincolnshire.

⚜ REPRIEVE FOR ONE-LEGGED MAN ⚜

Lincoln prison on Greetwell Road, north of the city, has experienced some amazing events in its history, including the stunning escape of Irish premier Eamon de Valera, in February 1919. But one of the strangest stories is surely the scene in the gaol in November 1954 when John Docherty was told that he would not hang. He was in the condemned cell awaiting his fate at the hands of the executioner, for the murder of his fiancée, Sybil Hoy, in Grantham. What was peculiar about all this was that Docherty had lost both legs as he tried to take his own life on the track in front of a train. Both legs were severed but he survived.

Naturally, in such a case there would be a sensitive issue at the heart of the death sentence. Although it had taken only three minutes to delierate before sentence was passed, other factors were to emerge later. In cases of physical deformity, the notion of clemency and common humanity might apply, and a royal pardon be given. The reprieve finally came after the Home Secretary had reviewed the case file. In the end, the point to be debated was how a legless man could be hanged with dignity. In effect, it is the Home Secretary who can choose to exercise the royal perogative of mercy, on behalf of the Crown.

The circumstances of the murder are that John was engaged to Sybil while they were living in Felling, Durham. The future should have been bright, but (partly due to the unhealthy nature of the area they lived in) John contracted tuberculosis and had to be installed in a sanatorium. For a while it looked as though he had recovered; but at that time the prevailing fear and concern about the disease was dominated by the thought that someone with this illness would not really be wise to marry: it could go on through progeny, of course. John unfortunately suffered a relapse and was again hospitalised. The outlook was now sombre and very desperate; time went on and Sybil had other young men paying her attention. John was being left out of her life, and he began to pursue her, to the point of obsession and harassment. She tried to 'disappear' and be beyond contact. But he found her in Grantham and did some detective work to locate her in the town. Sybil was staying in Arnoldfield Flats. On the night of her murder, she walked out into the dark with the three-year-old child of her friend, little Kevin. A neighbour heard screams and ran to the area, only to discover that Sybil had been beaten and stabbed to death. It was a dramatic scene: the pushchair was upside down when the neighbour ran to see what was happening.

Docherty was crouching in nearby undergrowth, still with the knife in his hands, and he told the neighbour that he had stabbed her a few times. He then fled. She had, in fact, been stabbed no fewer than nineteen times. It was a frenzied attack by a man who was in a murderous rage of revenge.

Not far off, and a little later, Mr Ernest Bond was working with his colleagues, platelaying on the railway; they paused when a fast train, going at around 70mph, rushed past. Seconds after it had gone, Ernest saw something on the line: something he thought was a bundle of clothes. It was Docherty, and his legs had been sliced off. He was rushed to Grantham hospital and received all the attention he needed, but by 12 August the police were at his bedside, and he was charged with murder. In Grantham Guildhall,

Ernest Bond. Bond was the man who found Docherty after the horrific accident. (Illustration by Laura Carter)

which he entered in a wheelchair, he was charged and remanded in custody. In Lincoln, at the Assizes, he had made a full confession – not only to murder but to attempted suicide. The latter was a crime at the time, and was so until 1961. He pleaded guilty and was scheduled to hang on 23 November.

It was just eight days before that appointment with the scaffold that he was told about the reprieve. The file with 'Urgent – Capital Case' would have been placed in front of the Home Secretary, and he made a decision that the tabloids had been clamouring for over the previous weeks, as the date of execution was drawing nearer.

Back in 1907, some of the decisive factors in such decisions had been given by the then Home Secretary, Herbert Gladstone. He had said that, 'The motive, the degree of premeditation or deliberation, the amount of provocation, the state of mind of the prisoner, his physical condition, his character and antecedents... have to be taken into account in every case.' The judge may have had his own opinion at the time of the sentence, but that could not play a part in the passing of the sentence the criminal law demanded, regardless of the state of the man before him in the dock. Docherty stated that after Sybil left him, he 'did not want to live any more.' She had returned all kinds of presents he had given her, and of course, she had returned his engagement ring. That would have been the final blow. He had no reason to go on living, and his twisted mind thought that she should not live either.

The other factor, however – and it is a very delicate though practical one – is that the professionals who would have had to deal with Docherty in the execution suite at the prison would have been asked to go through a demeaning experience. The prison officers, the chaplain, the governor and indeed the hangman would have found the notion of hanging a legless man not only absurd but unethical. As to whether the man was of sound mind at the time of the killing – well, yes. He had planned to murder Sybil. But the 'system' could not cope with the responsibility of granting his second wish, to die, and the media played a part in that dilemma.

Docherty was not the only case reprieved that year: in 1953, five of the eighteen people sentenced to die were reprieved. As to Docherty's sentence, he was to serve not less than fifteen years. The most relieved man in Lincoln on that day when the long-awaited news arrived at HMP Lincoln was surely the governor, William Harding. As to the hangman, he must have been delighted that he had been deprived of the practical problem of how one pinions such a man, and how the 'drop' would be calculated accurately.

If we look for comparisons to this strange tale and the act of taking men to execution who are ill or in some way unfit to face the experience, perhaps the strongest parallel is a political one, because in Kilmainham gaol, Dublin, after the Easter rebellion of 1916, James Connolly was taken out to face a firing squad; he was on a stretcher and had been taken from a bed in the Castle Hospital before he was carried into the stone-breaking yard to be despatched to the next world. The comparison only serves to illustrate that, when it comes to trying to understand the nature of capital punishment through modern eyes, there is no point in looking for consistency in the routes by which men and women arrived at their fatal appointments at the hands of the state. The inconsistent and often brutal chronicle of twentieth-century capital punishment will always be found to have dozens of stories like this of Docherty: at the centre of these dramas there are always the circumstances of the individual case, and this is invariably at odds with the letter of the law. Not only did questions of insanity and sanity raise difficult moral issues in court, but contrasts of crimes performed in different 'arenas' of crime caused problems.

Not surprisingly, in this case the popular media made a sensation of the affair, and in the annals of murder this will always be simply known as the 'legless man story'. Beneath this, however, there is a desperately melancholy tale of a man – like Othello – who loved, 'Not wisely, but too well' and jealousy led to the old formula for the crime of passion: 'If I can't have her, then nobody else will either.'

S

⁕ SHEELA-NA-GIGS ⁕

Writing in his classic architectural guide in 1964, Niklaus Pevsner had only a page of notes on the St John the Baptist church at Great Hale. He noted, writing about one particular feature: 'The south window has some defaced decoration round the arch.' What he did not know was that this very old church, with its Saxon tower, contained some very old carvings of a sexual and symbolic nature, found almost everywhere but of Gaelic origin, called *sheela-na-gigs*. The great architectural historian Gerald Baldwin-Brown had found such a figure in the church and he made a drawing.

The sheela is usually a woman with a prominent vulva, or a male figure holding his penis. Clearly, these are fertility symbols, as are found in cultures across the world. The sexual representation is grotesque and humorous as a rule; the carvings often show torso and ribs, and the figures are usually found in Norman or Romanesque churches. They are found in all regions of Britain. There is a national sheela-na-gig project underway to try to gather all the diverse information about the carvings.

Recently, Paul Everson and David Stocker have written about this Lincolnshire sheela. As they explain, Baldwin-Brown, working in Great Hale, made a drawing of a figure there: 'Baldwin-Brown had sketched a second carved figure at Great Hale, noting its location in the interior arch of the western double belfry opening of the tower. Brown's drawing seems to show a naked male figure with a raised right arm set within an arched panel.'

In England, sheelas date from the twelfth century, and were in bordered panels; the Great Hale one has been re-cut to be used inside the church at the head of the belfry. The tantalising question for historians is how this figure in Lincolnshire may have been made much earlier than the accepted date for the figures, but whatever the date, the point is that the figure was seen as morally offensive at the later date, when he was moved to the belfry. As Everson and Stocker point out, '... its original rationale was either lost or had become offensive to puritan mind-sets.'

⁝ SMUGGLERS ⁝

In 1690, down in Romney Marsh, the job role of Riding Officer was established. This meant that a man in uniform was to ride on patrol, covering several miles of coast, looking out for smugglers and contraband goods, vessels offshore and nefarious activities by moonlight. Of course, smuggling was a standard version of a local economy through the centuries, but something had to be done and the Riding Officer was just one of many measures implemented – one that did not work very well. The Riding Officer was always a victim. On the East Coast of Yorkshire, on one occasion, an officer had not been paid for three months and had to write to his master begging for his wages.

This byway of local history is one that existed alongside smuggling – a major business enterprise for a very long period. The shores of the Humber and the narrow river courses of North Lincolnshire were perfect smuggler territory. In the seventeenth and eighteenth centuries it was rife. In the 1700s there was a large excise duty on such luxuries as tea and tobacco, so a black market inevitably grew. But there are case studies from much earlier, such as that of William de Len and his gang from Louth, who, in the thirteenth century, sold 200 sacks of wool to merchants over the North Sea, taking them over with the aid of bribes.

In the ancient records of the Court of Star Chamber, a court that in Tudor times was to restrain 'over-mighty subjects' and deal with everything from sedition to top-class theft and assault, there are accounts of Humber pirates. Remarkably, one documented story of these villains links to the Abbot of Whitby. The Abbot in the late sixteenth century had dealings with a gang described by one early writer as doing 'questionable transactions'. Little more is known about some mysterious crooks called Ganth, Lappage and Parys, but in a 'ring' with the Abbot and with a powerful local magnate called Conyers, they plied their trade.

The man called Ganth was arraigned for carrying, among other goods, something called 'osmonds' and the antiquarian Edward Peacock suggests that these were 'the very best iron used for the finest purposes such as arrow-heads, fish-hooks, the repairs of bell-gear and the works of clocks.' Garth was going to get very rich on this trade of osmonds along the Humber. After docking in the Humber, his French colleagues shipped

Old postcard of Whitby Abbey, whose Abbot once ran a ring of smugglers.

materials up the coast to the Abbot. It was all very lucrative, until the Star Chamber men found out. There is no record of what the punishment was, but we know that the officers of the Chamber put pressure on jurors to ignore the truth and find guilt where the desire to convict was strong. The Tudor monarchs hated the thought of any other faction or group having any degree of power that might be too grand, and smuggling was a way to enjoy that status.

Smuggling and piracy were often so large-scale an enterprise that the authorities could do nothing to prevent them. In the early sixteenth century, there were so many Scottish ships at the Humber estuary that local captains were afraid to set out to sea; there would be a ransom to be paid if they did. There were also local squabbles. On one occasion two merchants fell out and one slandered the other by saying that the 'false wretch' had hidden away sheep skins and not paid duty on them – many men were found out, of course. One historian recorded a number of offenders who had been breaking the law on a grand scale:

> ... it was ascertained by a jury, impanelled for the purpose, that Roger de Brigsley had shipped six sacks of wool, of the value of seven marks per sack, at the port of Grimsby for export into Flanders ... and that William Sevenac at the same time sent five sacks of wool in sheets, price eight marks each ... and at Easter he smuggled five sacks more.

Even with the arrival of an efficient coastal excise patrol in the nineteenth century, smugglers abounded, such as Thomas Lumley who was fined the massive sum of £1,500 in 1826 for smuggling. He would store his goods in a barn at Stallingborough and then take them to Aylesby Church where he would use the tower to keep them. It has been suggested that the name New Holland derives from his trade in illicit gin, because the old name for gin was Hollands gin or, in Dutch, *Hollandsch genever*.

In 1869, a gang comprising George Atkinson, Stephen Andrews, Edwin Bray and Palmer Bray were charged with smuggling. The accused were all firemen on the steamship, *Grimsby*. A customs officer called Mumby boarded the ship before she left for Hamburg. When he went into the engine-room he found sixty packages of tobacco in a waste-locker. It was his second search of the vessel and maybe, at that point, he would have been satisfied that the men were just working on a moderate level of petty crime.

However, the tobacco had been kept in some waterproof tin cases and so Mumby's suspicions were aroused. Consequently he pumped under the boiler and there he found a space of 2ft between the boiler and the framework of the ship; only by going under the boiler could the goods have been taken out, and more goods were found concealed within.

The culprits were given a heavy fine of £100 and were ordered to be kept in Lincoln Castle prison until the fines were paid. That was a huge sum of money at this time, and the papers reported, some weeks after, that the fines were not paid. Mumby had done some detective work and spotted that some trousers and a Guernsey sweater had had tobacco packed in them and stuffed under the boiler as well.

Such cases were common, and the usual view was that the risks were worth the potential profits. Mumby's occupation was a lot more secure and prestigious than that of the poor Riding Officer, anyway.

☙ SPRING-HEELED JACK ❧

In 1938, a Lincoln man named Rollins wrote to the local paper to tell readers that Spring-Heeled Jack had been in Lincoln. He wrote: 'In 1877 I lived at a farm in Newport. In that winter Spring-Heeled Jack came to Lincoln and jumped over Newport Arch… the young men of the town used to come out and try to catch him.'

This mysterious street prowler had been supposedly seen in England's streets since the autumn of 1837, when he appeared in London. Most accounts of this rogue, who used to assault people at night, agree that he wore a black cape and a bat-like cap. He was supposed to have had springs in his shoes, enabling him to jump 20ft in the air.

A witness in Old Ford, near London, in 1838, said that Jack appeared in the dark street and asked for a light before shoving and robbing the man. He often used claws on his fingers to tear clothes before stealing from his victims. One alleged victim, Lucy Scales, was said to have had flames spat at her by him. All through the nineteenth century he appeared in all kinds of places, or so the legend goes. Some of the appearances were closer to what we now call 'happy slapping' than anything else. So powerful was this mythic figure in the popular imagination that, in 1888, when Jack the Ripper was about in Whitechapel, some thought both Jacks were one and the same.

Jack looked something like a prototype for Batman. He had a cape and a mask, with allegedly spiralled springs in his shoes that allowed him to jump 15ft in the air. There is a theory that, because of a crest on his cape, he was the Marquis of Waterford.

Richard Whittington-Egan, writing about Jack, noted other locations and also descriptions of him, referring to what some soldiers had seen of Jack in Aldershot camp. It is interesting to note that the soldiers' description of what they saw – a tall, thin figure wearing a tight-fitting suit and gleaming helmet, with glowing red eyes and blue flames issuing from its mouth – was couched in terms amazingly similar to those use by Jane Alsop forty years before (in London).

In Lincoln, the description was that Jack's costume was like a sheepskin with a peculiar tail and he was said to have huge, pointed ears. At least two shots were fired at him, but he always escaped over roof-tops.

⚛ STAMFORD SPA ⚛

In the Victorian years, towns across the land worked hard to emulate the successful spa towns which had been earlier established; Bath and Scarborough, for instance. Places such as Ilkley and Malvern developed their water treatment and notable medical men realised the commercial potential of these places, where the wealthy patients would come to 'take the waters'. In 1819, Stamford tried to cash in on this fashion.

Stamford Spa
stone. (Drawing by
Vicki Schofield)

At that date, there was an ironstone spring for mineral waters –
apparently much respected and used. In 1864 a man called John Paradise
placed a stone head on the spot as a memorial.

Technical details include the information that the water contained
oxide of iron, carbonate of lime, muriot of soda (an older word for
chloride) and sulphate of lime.

❧ STONE STORIES – WINCEBY AND FONABY ❧

Stones and rocks have always been at the heart of folk tales across the
world, perhaps the most famous being 'The Sword in the Stone' and the
Arthurian legends. But much more modest are the tales of local stones
and their traditions. At Winceby, famous for the Civil War battle there,
there is the Winceby Boulder. Ethel Rudkin, in the 1930s, explained that
it stood near Slash Hollow and was supposed to guard hidden treasure.
The tradition was that it could never be moved but on one occasion a
farmer tried to do so, and Ethel relates that after moving it, something
strange happened:

> The stone moved in its bed and looked like coming out altogether, when one of
> the men helping said, 'Let God or the Devil come now, for we have it!' Something
> appeared to be standing on the stone, and it seems to have been the Old Lad himself,
> for he left his claw-mark on the stone in evidence.

There was another effort to move the stone and that time a black mouse ran out and scared the horses, who would never go there again. Eventually the stone was buried in a massive hole.

The sack stone at Fonaby near Caistor was on the north-west corner of a field on a hill above the village. It possibly had a practical use, according to Ethel, who wrote about several stones across the county. A retired farmer explained to her that, 'When sowing corn by hand a sack is placed so many yards from either fence at the opposite sides of the field, the distance in the middle between the sacks being double the distance from a sack to the fence, so that the hopper is filled and lasts from the sack to the fence.'

There was supposed to be a curse on the stone, however, to be put on anyone who moved the stone away, but it was at times rolled a short distance to test out the curse, and no one suffered. Eventually it was considered to be a nuisance when it came to ploughing the field and it was towed away to a yard, and there it was used by cattle that stood on it to reach the water-trough. But Ethel recalled that a farmer reported bad consequences, saying that his horses died and his son was ill. Apparently the stone was dragged back into its former place and all was well.

But allegedly, a later farmer on the land, who had worked it for twenty years before he spoke to Ethel, said that he had the stone shifted to the edge of the field and 'three horses died within the week.' Later, the stone split, and the conclusion was that 'the power seemed to go'.

Boulders and prehistoric standing stones have always attracted legends, of course. Even as late as the nineteenth century, many people in country areas thought that they grew in the soil and rose to the surface. In one reference work we have this comment: '… many countrymen insisted it was no use having stones picked off one's fields because the land produced them, and there would soon be as many as ever. This was still being said in Staffordshire in the 1960s.' (*Oxford Dictionary of English Folklore*)

❖ STOW SWINEHERD ❖

Sometimes a figure from history comes down to us more vividly in a satirical story than in the record of facts and achievements. That may well be the case with Robert Bloet, one of the early Bishops of Lincoln. It is known that he died in 1123 but his date of birth is uncertain. He became Chancellor under William the Conqueror and then was given the see of Lincoln, where he made his mark. He was always embroiled in some kind

A picturesque Victorian view of Lincoln Cathedral, where a carved figure of Bloet may be seen. (Library of Congress, Prints & Photographs Division, LC-DIG-ppmsc-08547)

of trouble, even in a row with Thomas of Bayeux, Archbishop of York, who wanted to Lindsey for his own York jurisdiction.

Bloet won the day, allegedly with the help of a vast sum of money from Bloet, oiling the palms of the right people. It may be that the so-called figure of a man blowing a horn on the north pinnacle of the west front of Lincoln Cathedral is Bloet. The old tale is that the swineherd gave a peck of silver pennies towards the building of the cathedral, and that may be a distortion of the Bishop's antics in bribery. Bloet was known to be something of a rake; he was a married bishop, but was said to be a tearaway, a wastrel and not really of the right moral fibre to be a bishop at all.

It may be that the grotesqueness of the swineherd face is a cheeky caricature of the Bishop. In the first reference to the swineherd, in a book by Charles Wild published in 1819, the word 'grotesque' is used to describe the face. If it is meant to be Bloet, then perhaps this is a sideways sweep at the man, who after all was in trouble to the very last, later being involved in lawsuits and being disgraced under Henry I.

In terms of art, and artistic reference to actual life, the very fact that the swineherd has a horn is odd. Such men usually need boards and sticks to move their swine and keep control. The fact that he has a horn is in itself a joke. It appears that the creator of this image was just as much a joker, in the fine tradition of English caricature, as Rowlandson or Cruikshank.

𝒯

⁙ TENNYSON'S BOGGARD ⁙

J.C. Walter, writing in 1904, recounts the tale of a ghost at Stainby. He spoke to a former resident of the village, and the man remembered, as he said in dialect, 'Well, when I were young I lived in them parts and I heard o' one oftens. I never seen it mesen but I knowed several who did.'

The ghost was often seen at a spot around half a mile from Somersby, close to the ash planting area. A wagoner who lived in Bag Enderby saw what he recalled as a 'misty kind of a thing', which 'flitted unaccountably'.

This ghost was not only noticed by locals: the tale reached the Poet Laureate, Lord Tennyson, who wrote of a farmer that was so bothered by this spirit that he harnessed his horse and cart and set off to escape the thing. Tennyson wrote:

> The farmer, vext, packs up his bed,
> And all the household stuff and chairs,
> And with his boy betwixt his knees, his wife
> Upon the tilt – sets out and meets a friend,
> Who hails him, 'What, are't flitting?'
> 'Yes, we're flitting' says the ghost,
> For they had packed her among the beds
> Oh well,' the farmer says, 'You're flitting with us too.'
> Jack, turn the horse's head home again!

This story is linked to a whole genre of ghost tales, notably in Wales but also elsewhere, about the boggards who come to haunt a farm and will not go away. In the folk tales they always somehow stay with their victims, who have to try to sneak away while the boggards are otherwise occupied. Maybe, in this case, legend is mixed with supposed fact.

In Tennyson's poem of 1842, 'Walking to the Mail', the treatment of the story is light-hearted: 'But his house so they say / was haunted by a jolly

Lord Tennyson.

ghost that shook / the curtains, whined in lobbies, tapt at doors / and rummaged like a rat. No servants stayed …'

The old man, interviewed by Mr Walter, had no doubts about the 'flitting thing' though. Maybe it's still seen today in that place. Tennyson could not resist a local tale, and he had both the humour and the genuine interest in the paranormal to use the tales on his doorstep.

❧ THORNTON ABBEY CORPSE ☙

The imposing remains of Thornton Abbey, not far from Barton, give testimony to the rapacious doings of Henry VIII, as it was one of the casualties of his depredations on the religious house of that time. But the beautiful place has something dark inside – very possibly the villain Dean Fletcher, and also there could be the uneasy ghost of an abbot who was killed by Dean there.

In the late fourteenth century, the Abbot, Thomas de Gretham, was enjoying a liaison with his student, Heloise. In a complex plot involving the Abbot, a tough who was known locally as the Green Devil and a stolen deed of land ownership, we have an awful tale of terrible punishment being inflicted on the Abbot by Fletcher. Fletcher is reckoned to have

The Great Seal of Henry VIII, including hunting hound, Tudor rose and the famous motto of the Order of the Garter.

felt the need to punish the religious man for 'lax living' and his particular form of punishment was to immure the Abbot inside the walls of the abbey.

In the 1830s, workmen found a secret room where there was a skeleton on the floor, which turned to dust when touched. It was wearing a monk's habit and looked like the unfortunate Abbot. However, there are other candidates for the identity of those remains. A report written in 1935 talks of a certain Walter Munton, who was also spoken of as 'an evil liver'; it is possible that the corpse may have been his. As with most of Britain in Tudor times, there was a threat of social anarchy most of the time, and these remains may well have been the victims of that supposed 'Green Devil' men spoke of at Thornton then.

The findings were reported in full in *The Gentleman's Magazine* in 1836:

> Adjoining the entrance to the chapter-house is an arched room, with pointed recesses for seats, after the manner of cathedrals. This apartment has no door, which is evident from the present remains, and was entered from the cloisters; by some, it has been stated to be the secret council chamber …

The curling signature of Henry VIII.

The ruins of Thornton Abbey, where ghosts are said to walk. (Photograph by David Wright)

The editor added the note that the reporter at the time, a Mr Greenwood, had described the chamber in detail, but that, 'If it was anything more than a portion of the cloisters, we cannot explain it; but the monks would certainly require no place of council more secret than their own chapter-house.'

In more recent times, visitors have spoken of being pushed or having heard whispers as they walk in the abbey; one correspondent has written that he 'felt a sudden sense of being overwhelmed with sadness' while standing there in the room over the arch, and that he had to leave the place immediately. This is backed up by other visitors talking of seeing shadows where there should be none and sensing movement in areas where they know that no other people have entered.

⚜ TOM OTTER AND THE GIBBET ⚜

Local ghost-hunting groups, most recently the researchers from Bassetlaw, have spent nights on the premises of the Sun Inn, at Saxilby, just outside Lincoln, close to Doddington Hall. This is because some reckon that this particular pub is the most haunted one in England, due to its link to one of the most brutal and callous murders ever committed

in Lincolnshire: Tom Otter's (otherwise known as Thomas Temporel)
murder of his new wife. Like so many aspects of the Otter story, we are
not sure where the truth lies.

But what we can be certain of are the facts of the murder, although
the details of the key witness to this are troublesome. The witness, John
Dunkerly, a labourer from north of Drinsey Nook towards the village of
Harby, had enjoyed a night at the Sun in November 1805. Talk must have
been dominated by the Battle of Trafalgar, only two weeks before this,
and other topics relating to Napoleon and Nelson. It was a long night, and
Dunkerly had to walk home, several miles through dark, lonely moorland.

Earlier accounts of Dunkerly, based on a long statement he made in
court, suggest that he was a 'peeping Tom' who made a habit of walking
out to lonely spots in search of courting couples. But he may have simply
been tired, stopping at a field corner and falling asleep. Whatever the
facts of the actual circumstances, he saw Tom Otter and his wife, Mary
Kirkham, together and he reported that Otter had sat her down and said,
'Sit down, you can rest here.' Then he walked into the undergrowth and
grabbed a hedge-stake. This was on 3 November, the day he had married
Mary at South Hykeham; she was pregnant by him and of course, he was
forced to marry, under pressure. But now, in the darkness, thinking they
were alone, he said, 'This will finish my knob-stick wedding' ('shotgun
wedding' in modern terms). It certainly did. Dunkerley saw everything.

Dunkerly was a casual labourer, and on that day he had taken some
time off, sitting in the Sun. At that time the pub would have been open
from half-past five in the morning through until midnight. Dunkerly left
his friends around six o'clock and started the long walk. His statement
claims that he passed two men he knew near Drinsey Nook, and that they
said, 'You'll have company, John.' They referred to the newlyweds, and
this may have given rise to the image of Dunkerly as a man who scouted
around for titillating, vicarious pleasure in his voyeurism.

If he was in a thick hedge, then Otter came very close to him as he
chose the hedge stake. Then, as Dunkerly describes, he noted that comedy,
not tragedy, began:

> The moon shined on his face at the time and his eyes frightened me, there was such
> a fiery look in them… Then he climbed down to where she was sitting with her
> head hanging down, and he swung the hedge stake with both hands and hit her a
> clout on the head. She gave one scream and called on God for mercy, then tumbled
> over with her head on the ground.

Dunkerly's account is convincing and graphic in its details; he even noted that Mary's body was 'all a-quiver like' before she became rigid. He described the second blow as being like hitting a turnip. With remarkable self-control, Dunkerly kept his silence, but it seems as though he passed out. When he awoke, the stake was near him, and there was some of Mary's blood on the sleeve of his smock.

The witness panicked at this and took to wandering around the area for a while, not knowing what to do – but the body was found and Otter was arrested. He was discovered at the Sun Inn, the same place that the body was taken after being found, and also the venue of the inquest. Here begins the kind of detail that led to the tale of Tom Otter becoming a standard Lincolnshire ghost story: blood dripped from Mary's body onto the steps of the Sun. The hedge stake was kept at the inn, as a piece of customer interest and good local 'spin' for attracting travellers who had an interest in gruesome stories.

The trial at Lincoln Castle was of one Thomas Temporel. But whether he was Temporel or Otter, we don't know. One of the key facts, though, is that he had married before this – to a woman in Southwell. Naturally, Otter would have had to pay for the maintenance of his new wife and child as well as for his existing wife. It is easy to see the problem from his standpoint, but the remedy was the most extreme one imaginable.

His trial lasted for five hours, with Justice Graham presiding. It cannot have been worse than the inquest, where poor Mary's corpse had been

Doddington Hall, where parts of the gibbet may still be seen. (Photograph by Peter Church)

laid out for all to see, with the gore-stained hedge stake nearby. Otter sentenced to hang, and his body was to be gibbeted. This was the practice of hanging the corpse of a murderer high above a road for all the birds to peck and consume, as a warning to others to keep to the law. A gibbet was a high post with an arm out, from which either the entire corpse or a limb would be placed. By the end of the eighteenth century, this was becoming a rare practice, but in the Otter case, his deed was so reprehensible that some horrible symbolic token of justice was needed. Otter was hanged in March 1806 and the irons and gibbet for him were made by a Saxilby man, the blacksmith, Dick Naylor. Otter was 'stretched' on Cobb Hall tower at the corner of the castle; the great bell, known as Great Tom, struck twelve.

Then the legends began. When the gibbet was raised into position, the weather was severe and there was a strong wind. After all, it was 30ft high and was raised by block and tackle. As an earlier writer, Thomas Burke, wrote in 1933, 'Nature seemed to be on the side of the murderer.' This was because the beam broke twice, and at one point the metal tackle fell down on the labourers. When it was all done, the story is that Dunkerly said, 'Well, he won't come down no more' – but, on the contrary, Tom Otter's remains then fell down on him.

The east gate of Lincolnshire Castle. (Photograph by Richard Croft)

The saga of the hedge stake is at the heart of the legend. It was supposed to go missing on 4 November every year, even though it had been being fixed to the wall. This still happened on the next anniversary. Finally, the Sun landlord sent it to the Peewit Inn not far away. A blacksmith used six clamps to fix this to a wall, but it went missing again. The end of this fantastic tale is that the stake was ceremonially burned by the walls of Lincoln Cathedral, by order of the Bishop himself.

John Dunkerly, whether we want to believe him or not, had undergone far more trauma, as a result of his witnessing the murder, than anyone knew until, as he lay dying, he told a tale of a terrible haunting to the minister who came to his bedside, including appearances by the ghost of Tom Otter himself. Dunkerly explained that the worst torments were on the anniversary nights of the murder:

I felt doley-like so I went to bed about dusk-hours, and what I'm trying to tell you is as true as that I'm a dying man. I couldn't nohow sleep and all of a sudden Tom Otter stood in front of me in his chains, and he says, 'It's time. Come along.' And I had to go with him. And he says, 'Fetch it. Make haste.' And I broke into the Sun Inn and fetched the hedge stake from off the nail... when I got outside the door, they were both waiting for me.

The gibbet stayed there until around 1850. Parts of this terrible object may still be seen by visitors to Doddington Hall. But the myth goes on: the judge, Basil Neild, writes in his memoirs about the case, and he recalls a rhyme written as a riddle, composed by an anonymous local poet:

10 tongues in one head
9 living and one dead.
One flew forth to fetch some bread
To feed the living in the dead.

Five Lane Ends, Harby, where the murder of Mary took place. (Photograph by Richard Croft)

The answer? Of course, it's 'The tomtit that built in Tommy Otter's head.'

The myth of Tom Otter (or Temporel) will go on and on, as it has all the elements of a folk tale and enough to keep people awake by the fireside when they are in the mood for a ghost story. Even today, at the Sun Inn, it is hard to avoid the sense of this dark and brooding past in that wild place that it was when Tom was there.

In Saxilby today, there is still much to see and to imagine in relation to the terrible tale of Tom Otter and his new wife.

$\mathcal{U}$

❧ UNCLE HICKY ❧

Sir Hickman Bacon is perhaps best remembered as one of the founder members of the Lincolnshire Automobile Club. He was president of that organisation from 1902 to his death in 1945. His first car was a Panhard Levassor, known around Gainsborough, where he lived, as 'The Dustbin'. It was noisy and was, of course, considered to be dangerous. After all, there had been casualties of motoring even before the end of the nineteenth century. There had been the first police car chase in England in 1899 and the first conviction for drink driving in 1897, so cars were dangerous things.

But 'Uncle Hicky' was a character and he was clearly held in great affection. He not only drove cars but invented items as well, such as a tyre lever he concocted, bought by the Dunlop firm. But arguably his greatest achievement was his exploits with Austin cars. From 1908 onwards he was keen on Austin racers, and of course he had to race. There is a tale that, because he had to acquire the requisite skills, he would drive at top speed from Caenby Corner to Lincoln (about twelve miles) with men placed along the route with flags.

He owned several Austins in his life, and he was a familiar figure to all around Gainsborough, being a lovable attraction for local children.

He was always very much involved in motoring affairs in the widest sense. In 1909, for instance, he attended the Road Conference in London and there he spoke on the topic of 'limiting the scope of irresponsible drivers' and on methods of raising funds for the condition and maintenance of arterial roads. In 1910 he added his name to a list of dignitaries who praised the Wolseley-Siddeley company, and in 1905 he was the victim of a threatening letter.

A man called Charles Kershaw wrote to 'Uncle Hicky' demanding with menaces the sum of £200. The man ended up in court in Lincoln. The report of the trial stated: 'The prisoner had sent a letter in 1893 demanding £500, threatening that if his demand was not complied with he would bring certain charges of the gravest nature against him.' He had then done a similar thing and Hicky had had enough. The judge said that the accused had sent letters 'of a cowardly and abominable nature' and that ten years of penal servitude would not be too harsh. He actually passed a sentence of five years. This was the only time Hicky was in the news for anything other than pleasant motoring matters.

If a story had to be found that typified his spirit and panache it has to be the supposed rivalry with John Sandars: they both yearned to have the first registered vehicle after the 1903 Motor Car Act and they allegedly tossed for that distinction in a hotel in Lincoln. 'Uncle Hicky' lost.

In some ways, he was a bit like the famous 'Mr Toad' and a bit of the typical British amateur sportsman of that age of adventure and enterprise. His name will always live on as long as there is The Lincolnshire Louth Motor Club, because they remember the man on Sir Hickman Bacon Day every year. He was surely one of the most outstanding personalities in the county's history, and there is always a need for men like him in every community.

⚜ VAN DIEMAN'S LAND ⚜

The convict tales told earlier are just a few from thousands. In many ways, Port Arthur penitentiary, close to Hobart, became an outpost of Lincolnshire, in the sense that so many Lincolnshire people were destined to live and die out there across the globe. The first fleet to Australia left in the summer of 1787. In the 1830s, the years in which transportation peaked, there were 5,000 convicts transported each year. Over a fifth of these came from Lincolnshire. We know a lot about conditions on the journey from surgeons' logs, as in this example from Peter Cunningham: 'Two rows of sleeping berths, one above the other, extend on each of the lower decks. Each berth being six feet square and calculated to hold four convicts, everyone thus possessing 18 inches space to sleep in – an ample space too ...'

These are some typical entries in the records:

> Burrell, Francis age 20, sentence, life to New South Wales in 1817 on board the
> *Almora*.
> Brue, Robert age 25 sentence 14 years in Van Dieman's land on board *Lord Lynedock*.

The destination, Port Arthur, was on an isthmus, with no possibility of escape without great risks, either of being shot when swimming across the bay, being savaged by the dogs tied on the beach, or, of course, from starvation out in the bush. One note in a Tasmanian newspaper has this information: 'With regards to those described as bushrangers or outside the law, it should be appreciated that during the 1805-1808 period the food situation was very critical, encouraging some convicts to absent themselves from their normal duties and live in the bush, existing on whatever wildlife they could kill or catch.'

Everyone was alert to the dangers of these convicts on the loose, as this note from the *Hobart Mercury* of 1854 notes:

The longed-for dream: a certificate of freedom from New South Wales, signed by the governor.

For some days past a tall, ill-looking fellow has been prowling about the neighbourhood of Glenorchy, committing depredations and escaping with impunity. On Sunday night he tried to break into the house of Mr Watson… fortunately a constable was near and he fired at him… but without effect as the darkness of the night favoured his escape.

What crimes had these Lincolnshire folk committed? Common offences were theft of goods and animals or assaults. Teenagers were sent to Van Diemen's Land for many years, and the only course of action open to relatives was to petition for mercy, as in this extract from a letter written by the mother of a young man:

I hope your Lordship will excuse the liberty I have taken of again writing to you respecting my son Henry Holland, now under sentence of transportation. Oh my Lord, if it be possible save my child from going abroad. This was his first offence, and consider his youth. Could you see the letter of penitence he has brought to me, the afflicted mother, I believe you would… show mercy.

∻ WESLEY'S FATHER IN DEBTORS' PRISON ∻

Today, a walk around the interior of Lincoln Castle and its prison buildings gives little idea of what the Georgian prison would have looked like. But part of that prison remains, built by the great John Carr, who worked on the exterior. Inside, the place was designed by William Lumby, a Lincolnshire man. In that inner sanctum would have been the Governor, his relatives, and the debtors of the county. In 1705, one of the inhabitants of that awful place was Samuel Wesley, father of the more famous John, then rector of Epworth, north in the Isle of Ancholme.

This fact might come as a shock to some, as it is easy to imagine the country life of a local churchman as being peaceful and comfortable, as he would receive plenty of local help, and would have his own plot of land (his glebe) on which to keep pigs or hens, or even grow vegetables. Samuel did have some of these things, but the problem was that he made enemies in his own parish, and these were so fierce and intractable that they virtually ruined him.

Both Samuel and his wife Susannah had blood links with nobility, and Samuel's Dissenter roots had brought him a good education and useful contacts. He aspired to write and to travel, and was always full of plans and schemes on a grand scale; at one time he seriously put forward a career move that involved disseminating religious knowledge and faith in India. He was always looking out for a more comfortable income, as his family was large, but he had a knack of making enemies. In his first living, at Ormsby in South Lincolnshire, he had offended John Sheffield, Earl of Musgrave by throwing the peer's mistress out of the rectory when she was making a social call.

When the Wesleys moved to Epworth, Susannah had just had her sixth child; it was going to be hard, and Samuel took an extra living, bringing in the nearby village of Wroot. But Samuel's awkward, unyielding and argumentative nature even caused a split between man and wife: Susannah would not say 'amen' after a prayer to the King and he sulked, sleeping in another room. This was the man who was to find that not only his nature, but sheer bad luck, were to strike at him, despite his efforts to make progress in the world. Susannah, known as 'Sukey', was the daughter of the great scholar Samuel Annesley of London. She knew her doctrine and her Bible, but she also stuck to her principles. It was a marriage of two strong temperaments.

One of his actions, which was clearly intended to find favour in an age of patronage, was a poem in praise of Master Godolphin, a folio pamphlet. This got him noticed by the powerful faction of the Duke of Marlborough, the champion of the battle of Blenheim. Not only was Samuel made a chaplain of a regiment for this, but he was also promised a prebend (a payment from the cathedral ruling body making him a cannon); but both of these were to be lost in the terrible acrimony and vengeance wreaked on him after a political mistake.

Samuel's ruin started when he changed allegiances at a local election, first promising to support the representatives of the Dissenters, but then changing to support the Church party when he learned of the aggressive attitudes of the Dissenters towards the Church. When the electioneering and news of the rector's perceived turncoat decisions reached the Isle of Axholme, Samuel Wesley was in for a very hard time. When Samuel was visiting Lincoln, he first had a scent of trouble to come as he talked to

A view of Lincoln Castle prison, where Wesley was to be incarcerated, in the late nineteenth century.

Susanna Wesley.

S Wesley

a friend in the Castle Yard and was told that his own parishioners were hunting for him, and that one had said they would 'squeeze his guts out' if they found him. After this, a campaign of terror was launched against Wesley and his growing family in Epworth.

It started with a mob outside the rectory and pistols being fired; his children were frightened. He was then arrested for debt (initially for a sum of around £30). His flax at home was burned, the door of the rectory damaged, and his cows stabbed. There he was, locked up in Lincoln Castle, writing letters home, knowing that his own family were being half-starved and terrorised. In a letter, he gives an account of the arrest:

> On Friday last, when I had been christening a child at Epworth, I was arrested in my churchyard by one who had been my servant, and gathered my tithe last year, at the suit of one of Mr Whichcott's friends… the sum was not £30; but it was as good as five hundred. Now, they knew the burning of my flax, my London journey, and their throwing me out of my regiment had both sunk my credit and exhausted my money.

Yet even in the prison, Samuel kept busy and pressed on with good work. He writes about reading prayers twice a day and preaching on Sunday. He was as sociable as ever, 'getting to know' his 'gaolbirds' as he said, and writing to the Society for Promoting Christian Knowledge for some books to give away. The working of the law was simple and inflexible: a debtor stayed in prison until the debt was paid. But most men in Samuel's situation would have no hope of clearing the debt; at least he had some powerful allies. Making himself busy helping the less fortunate was indeed a charitable thing to do, as many of the poorer debtors would be there for very long periods, and some would be in irons. Things had not changed much by 1776, when the prison reformer, John Howard, noted that 60 per cent of prisoners in England's gaols were debtors.

Samuel Wesley by
A.H. Hyde.

The most horrendous experience of the whole sorry time must surely
be the desperately tragic events of Wednesday, 30 May 1705, when
a mob came to the rectory firing guns and drumming in the 'rough
music' tradition of English culture. They were under the window where
Susannah had given birth just a few weeks before. Samuel had taken
the child to a neighbouring woman who acted as nurse, but this nurse
lay over the baby and suffocated it in her sleep. When she woke up and
found the corpse, she panicked and ran, screaming with fear to Wesley
and giving the baby to his servants. Then, the end of this agonising event
came with the dead baby being given to its mother. As Samuel reported
it, the child was given to her 'before she was well awake', thrown 'cold
and dead' into her arms.

His debts totalled £300, a very large sum then. He wrote about his
problems to Archbishop Sharpe of York, and that good man helped him,
both with money and with petitioning for help. Samuel was in the prison
for approximately six months, after a Mr Hoar paid him £95 and the
Archbishop added more. Back in Epworth he learned how his wife had

survived; she had sent him her wedding ring while he was imprisoned, and he had sent it back, but somehow she fed the family and kept morale high enough to carry on. She had had no money at all, and the food was mostly the bread and milk yielded from her glebe. But the poor man with a sickly wife and eight children had pulled through.

A profound irony during this period was in the tale of one of Samuel's most nasty enemies, who suffered a terrible accident. This was Robert Darwin, who went to Bawtry fair and fell from his horse after he had drunk himself dizzy; his fall dislocated his neck and forced an eye from its socket. Susannah reported that Darwin 'lived till next day but never spoke more' and that this was an example of the 'severe justice of God'.

Samuel's life had always been both hard and eventful; he was orphaned when he was a child and then at school, in Newington Green, he had been a schoolmate of Daniel Defoe. It was at Oxford that he entered the Church of England. His other life, that of writer and poet, is not much known, but because much of his work was burned in a fire at the rectory, it is difficult to assess his ability, and we can only say that a few of his hymns will live on in Methodist worship.

He died in 1735, at the age of seventy-two, wanting his son John to succeed him in Epworth. John, brother Charles and their friends travelled to Epworth to see Samuel before he died, as his time was near. Samuel's last words to his son Charles are memorable and typical of the man: 'Be steady. The Christian faith will surely revive in this kingdom. You shall see it, though I shall not.'

He may have been headstrong, and he was surely opinionated, but one thing is certain about Samuel Wesley: he went through hell on earth at that time; such were his truly awful trials and stresses.

⅏ WHERE DID THE TRAIN GO? ⅏

There is no doubt that some mishaps are not done with a purposeful desire to do someone, or something, harm. But nevertheless, painful and often tragic consequences can follow a piece of bungling in public service or even in relationships in a neighbourhood. This applies to a case against the Manchester, Sheffield and Lincolnshire Railway in which a passenger had a very hard time. The problem was that at the time the idea of negligence seemed to be a new concept.

There was a rich assembly of barristers on the Midland Circuit on 19 March 1862, to hear what had happened to Mr Burgess, a butcher and cattle dealer as he boarded a train for Grimsby after attending the Wakefield cattle market on Boxing Day, 1860. He was roughing it, travelling third class, and at that time trains were still something fairly new, so the notion of comfort was still in progress as well. Burgess had to change trains at East Retford and he went into a carriage next to the break-van, as was the normal way. He went into the middle compartment of three, together with six other passengers. That was just the beginning of his adventure.

An important detail here was that the communication cord, leading from Burgess's carriage to the break-van, had been taken out for some reason. The first stage of the journey was fine, stopping at Gainsborough and then on to Blyton. But there was snow on the line and the train was losing time; it was also snowing intensely. That snow was gathering deeply on the railway line.

Then the problems began. *The Times* reported the beginnings of the awful events of that night: 'Soon after the train started the passengers in the last carriage perceived that it swayed with a very irregular motion, which increased as it proceeded; the doors were flung open, the lamp above them fell onto the floor, and it was soon perceived that a wheel of which the tyre was broken, had gone off the axle.' After that, the whole body of the carriage toppled and it trailed along the ground. The unfortunate passengers had to cling on for dear life, grasping anything they could to hold on to.

The doors of the carriage and some of the sides were then broken and flapping; there was debris falling on the people. Everyone else had fallen off before Burgess: he fell heavily and his head was wounded. Somehow, he and the others managed to get to their feet and walked back to Gainsborough from Blyton. A doctor was fetched for him as he arrived in a pitiable condition at the White Hart inn. It was two days before he could get back home to Grimsby. Burgess was very ill for a month, confined to bed by his doctor.

He prosecuted the firm for negligence, the cause being that the break-van was at the engine side of the carriage, so the end-carriage was most vulnerable in the event of an accident. It was Boxing Day: staff may have been enjoying their beers too freely. But the company argued in court that there was simply a problem with one wheel; they said that the frost caused the tyre to burst. They also argued that they could not have kept a watchful eye on the passengers had they been placed in any carriage 'unless out guards had kept their bodies outstretched from the windows on the entire journey north.'

The barrister defending the company reasoned that there should be a considerable reduction in the amount of the damages claimed. What at first appeared to be on the side of the company (after their lawyer had done his homework well) was that Burgess had suffered a stroke in 1857; that gave them leeway to claim that the man had a weak constitution. For Burgess, his lawyer, Serjeant Hayes, gave a logical and very emotional response but it was left to the judge, the Lord Chief Justice, Mr Justice Williams, to advise the jury. He made it clear that there were weaknesses in the defences put forward by the company; Burgess was awarded £100 damages, which was a considerably large sum in those days.

The company were always having such problems with passengers in that decade. In the same year, a young woman was travelling from Hull to Grimsby to see her uncle when, between Haborough and Stallingborough, the carriage she was in 'oscillated very much'. The woman was taken off the train after her legs went completely numb and taken to Grimsby on a special train. She appears to have made a claim for damages after the contraction of bronchitis, but the harm done to one of her knees by the action of the engine was the main concern. The defence was that a spring had broken in the engine – and that there was no material defect in its construction.

It must have seemed as thought the company would win that case, as it was not difficult to show that the plaintiff had a 'weak constitution'. However, what happened was that the defence demonstrated – rather too aggressively – that her injury was only severe because she delayed taking medical advice. With a young woman, apparently crippled, looking pathetically weak next to the wealthy and well-fed representatives of a major transport company, the jury found for the plaintiff. In other words, the young woman was awarded the huge sum of £400 damages. It transpired that the inspector, the man who should have examined the keys in the chairs before departure, had not done so. The reporter told his public at the time that, 'Many of the keys supposed to have been displaced were not really so, but were new keys, purposely not driven home into the chairs.'

The heart of the problem then was not the engine but the very chairs that the passengers were sitting upon. Naturally, a frail woman at the mercy of such vibrations would suffer great pain. It all makes sense today, in our world of hyper-sensitive customer care and rigid Health and Safety legislation, but in 1862, they were just beginning to learn the folly of neglecting such things. The Manchester, Sheffield and Lincolnshire Railway had a lot to learn. Running a railway, they were discovering, meant much more that attaching carriages to a locomotive and heading in the right direction.

⚜ WILLOUGHBY WILD MAN ⚜

In Spilsby church there is a strange monument to Richard Bertie and his wife, who was the heiress to the Willoughby d'Eresby estate. It has a hermit on one side and on the other a wild man. The origin of the coat of arms is the Bertie and Willoughy families, and the Earls of Abingdon in Oxfordshire. That link to Oxford gives us the main tradition of the wild man story.

In English folklore, the wild man figure (sometimes called a *wodewose*), with his long hair, belt of leaves and beard and horns, relates to several versions of the figure across the world, including the Silenus of Greek mythology and the Sasquatch in Canada. There are two conventional narratives of the wild man; one with him as a nasty figure, doing harm to anyone in his way, and the other is to quite benign creations that are in fact manifestations of the good spiritual side of nature in general. The wild man of the Willoughby memorial almost certainly relates to the story of the wild man of Orford, a tale about a man coming from the sea who was caught in a fisherman's net. This is why, in some images, he has a fish's tale, rather like a mermaid.

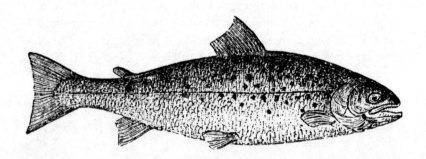

The Orford tale began with a story written by Ralph of Coggleshall in his work, *Chronicon Anglicanum* in 1200. This was preserved by the monks at Coggeshall Abbey in Essex. The wild man was supposedly captured and imprisoned at Orford castle, but he escaped.

There is no doubt that the modern investigations under the name of cryptozoology, in which expeditions go in search of the 'Bigfoot' and the Himalayan Yeti, are linked to the old image of the wild man in folklore.

The monument in Spilsby, in the Willoughby Chapel at St James Church, is to Richard Bertie, who died in 1582 and his wife, who was previously the Duchess of Suffolk, who died in 1580. The monument also has texts from the Bible in Latin and in English, on a panel. The wild man will continue to intrigue writers and folklorists for years to come. His identities range from wood spirit to weird creature and his presence on a coat of arms adds other fascinating questions about him; answers are perhaps shrouded in the mists of tradition and folk-memory.

⋅§ X-RATED POSTCARDS §⋅

Donald McGill was the artist who produced the famous 'saucy postcards' once found at all English seaside resorts. The humour of his cards was one of the treats of being on holiday and thousands of them were sent home by people who were relishing their time in the sun or in the pub. A typical card was one showing a scene in a bedroom in which a busty and scantily-clad blonde says to her lover, 'Blimey, here's my husband – can you come back tonight?' The man, looking suitably flushed and disturbed, is the stereotype milkman, and he replies, 'What in my known ruddy time – are you kidding missus!'

In the 1950s, McGill and his publishers were in trouble. The images and jokes were running into problems with the obscene publications legislation. He had experienced trouble before then, but not very often. McGill once said, with this trouble in mind, 'During the whole period of my career the authorities have made no complaints about the post cards drawn by me, with the following exceptions: in or about 1906 I recollect that an order was made for the destruction of a very large number of cards in the North of England; in or about 1920 proceedings were taken against the retailers of cards but no order was made.'

It comes as a shock to read about the problems in 1954, because McGill has the status of being recognised and complimented by no less a literary figure than George Orwell, who wrote an essay, 'The Art of Donald McGill' in 1941, and in a letter to Anthony Powell in 1947 was well aware of the likelihood of offence caused by the cards when he said, 'Thanks so much for your postcard which I think was rather lucky to get here – at any rate I think the crofter who brings the post the last seven miles might have suppressed it if he had seen it.' Orwell was living on the Isle of Jura, and he feared that the community there were too austere and morally righteous to accept the kind of ribald humour on a McGill card.

The grave of George Orwell
(Blair's pen name) in Sutton
Courtenay. (Photograph by Brian
Robert Marshall)

HERE LIES
ERIC ARTHUR BLAIR
BORN JUNE 25TH 1903
DIED JANUARY 21ST 1950

After the return to government of the Conservatives in 1951 there was
a moral reaction to the slippage in 'standards' of morality in the arts as it
was perceived at the time. In the five years following that date there were
167,000 books censored. It was only a matter of time before attention
turned to the saucy postcard. At the time there were 'watch committees'
at seaside resorts, and Cleethorpes was no exception. It was a regular
occurrence to have complaints voiced against such things as the postcards,
and many people considered them to be lewd rather than harmless fun. It
was inevitable that there would be police raids on premises where cards
might be in stock, and actions began to be taken in Grimsby. Police raids
resulted in the arrest and prosecution of both publishers and artists.

The Grimsby County Petty Sessional Division court issued writs on
behalf of the Director of Public Prosecutions, against merchants who
produced the McGill cards. The wording of the summons was 'unlawfully
published an obscene postcard named Donald McGill Comics
no. 811.' The Cleethorpes Chamber of Trade was worried too: in 1953
the Honorary Secretary wrote to Messrs D. Constance Ltd in London to
find out about the circulation and distribution of the cards, because as the
secretary wrote, 'Seventeen shops in the town were raided by the police.'
He added that, 'Quantities of comic cards were taken away, so no doubt

proceedings will follow to the annoyance to everyone of the traders concerned.' He wanted to know if the cards in Cleethorpes were typical of the merchandise going elsewhere. Obviously, if there were a set range of cards going to every town, then there would be a massive number of raids and potential prosecutions.

This legal action stemmed from the 1857 Obscene Publications Act. The outcome locally was a prominent trial in Lincoln on 15 July 1954. McGill's own defence was that in most of the images he had 'no intention of double meaning and in fact in some cases, a double meaning was pointed out to me.' He was found guilty and had to pay £50 in a fine and £25 in costs. Obviously, large amounts of cards were destroyed; many of the smaller postcard producers were ruined.

The onslaught against publishers and shopkeepers was relentless. In Brighton in July 1953, magistrates ordered the destruction of 113 out of 175 varieties of postcards. One of the defendants spoke up on behalf of the general grievances felt by seaside traders when he said, 'You are a kind of Arts Council on this matter.' One merchant conceded that the cards were sometimes 'a little near the knuckle', but the most that could be said in criticism was that there was an innuendo in the image and the text.

At that time, people in Cleethorpes had been more worried by recent floods and extremely bad weather, but the affair certainly disturbed the normal equanimity of the Cleethorpes traders. As for George Orwell, he had his own defence of McGill:

> The comic post cards are one expression of his point of view, a humble one, less important than the music halls, but still worthy of attention. In a society which is still basically Christian they naturally concentrate on sex jokes… Their whole meaning and virtue is their unredeemed lowness. They stand for the worm's eye view of life.

In other words, as with all humour of the baser kind, they remind us of the absurdity of moral strictness to the extent of denying communication about such topics as sex. But that view was too advanced for the austere world of 1950s Britain. With hindsight, it would be easy to see this case as a storm in a tea-cup – something rather more eccentric than important. But in fact the reasoning behind the bans was the significant factor. Here was a case in which a harmless and titivating ingredient of the English seaside experience was removed for the sake of 'decency' and of course today we are able to judge that in terms which seem unreal and distorted, because out modern political correctness has no room for what was then merely considered by most people to be 'saucy' in a way like the *Carry On* films.

The McGill case turned out to be little more than yet another instance of what Lord Macaulay called, sarcastically, a 'fit of morality': 'We know of no spectacle so ridiculous as the British public in one of its periodical fits of morality.' Naturally, at the time it brought out yet again the debate about what is art and what is smut. Only six years after this fiasco Britain would have to cope with the attempt to understand the *Lady Chatterley's Lover* trial. Like the McGill case, it would seem to many to be little more than victimisation, part of a 'jobsworth' attitude. Nevertheless, it is difficult today to bring to mind the kind of apprehensions felt by ordinary people, running their small business in such a strange moral climate.

𝒴

⊰ YARBOROUGH YARN ⊱

Sackville Lane Fox's father, Sackville Senior, was a yeomanry officer, the 12th Baron Conyers; he had three children with Mary Curteis and they had three children. Sackville, known as Sack or Jacko in the family, was born in London in 1861. In the autumn of 1878 he set off for Natal, with nothing planned regarding his soldiering there. He simply knew that he wanted to join a regiment and fight the Zulu. In a letter home in December that year he wrote, 'I am going on to Natal by the American tomorrow but don't know what I am to do there. Some people say I may get a commission in a levy and some say I may be attached as a volunteer with a British regiment. If I don't get something at once I shall join one of those irregular regiments.'

This points to one important aspect of the war immediately – a fact that Henry Curling commented on when he wrote that 'such numbers of officers are coming out here in search of fighting that they cannot think there is to be anything of the kind in Europe. We have got six officers in my battery now, of them senior to me and there are several other gunners waiting employment.' Sack was out for adventure and he was one of the many, as Curling saw. But the son of Lord Conyers had an introduction to Sir Bartle Frere, and just a short time before the Chelmsford columns advanced, he met Frere: 'Sir Bartle was very kind and asked me to dinner and offered me a room in the same house as his staff, and said he would do all he could for me – He introduced me to Major Mitchell.'

Sack joined the Natal Native Infantry and he noted that he was to cross the Tugela. His words when writing home are enlightening with regard to the attitudes at the time:

There will be a howling fight as the Zulus always come out in great masses and charge and of course they will shot down by the thousand, but after the first fight the fun will be over and the nasty work of hunting them in the bush will begin, as they will get such a lesson that they will not show their faces in the open… The soldiers here think they will shoot a thousand of them by Sunday.

The irony is huge, of course, but arguably these attitudes betray knowledge he heard: that is to say, that other men there had told a newcomer about the way the Zulu fight. These unwise attitudes were part of the Chelmsford mindset and were also the talk in the tents and mess rooms. Chelmsford had written to Theophilus Shepstone in July 1878 of the Zulu: 'They must be thoroughly crushed to make them believe in our superiority, and if I am called upon to conduct operations against them, I shall strive to be in a position to show then how hopelessly inferior they are to us in fighting power.'

But Sack Lane-Fox never moved further north than a dot on the map south of the Tugela; after Isandlwana, on 10 February 1879, he wrote home: 'I suppose you hear what an infernal mess we have got into. We have all bolted behind earthworks and until troops come out from England we shall never show our faces more than a mile or so from our trenches.' They had dug in and cowered, close to the river, and had not advanced because they could not gather a full complement of men. The other battalions had their full complement of 1,100 men but Sack's was short, with only officers and NCOs and three incomplete companies.

The intelligence was, by then, spreading with a mix of fact and rumour. Sack was told (we do not know by who) that there was a body of Zulu numbering 1,500 strong in the rear of their position. His force was just the 1st and 3rd battalions of the Natal Native Infantry. All they could do was 'get on top of a steep hill and make a fort… and we have had such a scare that we have not stopped digging yet.'

Sack and his men were clearly isolated. The picture we have here is of the sheer isolation and vulnerability of all scattered forces after the defeat. Sack's men he said, 'have such a holy fear of Zulus that if there is an alarm, which happens regularly twice or three times a week, they all bolt in every direction and it takes a day to get them together again.'

There was no communication and no information brought to them, wherever they were positioned. He did not know where he was. He wrote to his father, 'I don't put my address because the place has no name but it is somewhere on the frontier about 30 miles from a beastly little place called Greytown.'

All that could be done, in between the alarms, was drill. He noted, 'We have about 200 kaffirs and 60-70 whites – about 30 mounted. As to the weapons: some of the natives had Martini-Henrys and some had Sniders or Enfields, but mostly they had assegais and knobkerries. Sack's account of drill is done humorously, but it throws light on the amateurism and sheer mess of the forces behind the imperial infantry, engineers and so on, who had gone on to fight:

> The men with firearms go in the skirmish line and the assegai men form the reserve and when close enough to the supposed enemy are made to charge. It is the queerest charge imaginable… they run as fast as you can gallop and yell like mad and the ground is very steep and full of holes so some of them go over… the sergeants swear and all the horses bolt and altogether it takes about an hour to get the regiment together. Hardly any of us speak Kaffir.

In plain terms, this sheds light on the nature of the preparations Chelmsford and Frere had existing behind the main lines. Of course, the three columns sent forward and the two columns in reserve, at crucial points of protection and communication, were seemingly intelligently planned, and Chelmsford knew the priorities. However, what Sack Lane-Fox's letters home show is that in a large number of auxiliaries (and this was a war of second-liners and late arrivals) there was chaos and very little knowledge of the enemy. 'Hardly any of us speaks Kaffir', was something Wolseley would not have allowed.

Communication was hearsay. Sack notes that there was possibly a naval brigade 250 strong coming up along the bank and two companies of the 14th coming from Martizburg. Sack saw the reality of the situation: 'If we move anywhere by ourselves we must be smashed.' We have an insight into the terrain also, when he notes 'If the river goes down a little lower… the Zulus will cross and look us up.' All they could do was sit and wait, under arms every morning, from half past two. It rained most of the time and there was a mist. Sack commented, 'The sun comes out and takes all the skin off your hands and face and then sets fire to the grass.'

He soon wanted out of all that, writing to his father asking to get him leave 'even if it means resignation in my name.' He never saw a Zulu, and he died from dysentery in Durban on 28 August. His mother wrote to him, 'It is a great disappointment to us that you never 8 Zulu' [*sic*]. The last report on him was that 'he was very patient and brave to the last. He passed away without any effort or struggle.'

His father had pulled all the strings he could to get his son out to Natal. In September 1877 he had asked Willoughby Loudon to help and his friend replied, 'All the foreign applications seem to have fallen through. Lady Conyers has had no answer from Colonel Roberts.'

Z

❧ ZOO STORY: CLEETHORPES GIRAFFES ❧

For Z we have to look at a story from 1966. This is a tale of two giraffes which had to be taken to Cleethorpes Zoo from their place of arrival in the west by a special route. They had to by-pass Barnsley because that town had too many low bridges: Giraffes have to have a clearance of at least 15ft 5in. Their journey was twenty-five miles longer than the normal Manchester to Cleethorpes route.

The low bridges' lesson was not learned by a coach company in Leeds that year. One of their buses was stuck under a road-bridge on the way back from the Doncaster races. No giraffes were sighted anywhere else on the circuitous and undulating Yorkshire routes. The giraffes arrived safely in Cleethorpes and were the main attraction that year.

Lincoln river scene from the mid-nineteenth century.

Bibliography and Sources

✤ BOOKS ✤

Armstrong, A., *Lincolnshire Stories and Humorous Reminiscences* (Old Chapel Lane Books, 2007)

Brandon, D., *Rutland and Stamford Curiosities* (Dovecote Press, 2004)

Briggs, K., *British Folk-Tales and Legends* (Routledge, 1977)

Kettringham, J.R., *A Lincolnshire Hotchpotch* (The author, 1989)

MacGregor, A., *The Ghost Book: Strange Hauntings in Britain* (Robert Hale, 1955)

Pevsner, N. & Harris, J., *The Buildings of England: Lincolnshire* (Penguin, 1964)

Rawnsley, W J., *Highways and Byways in Lincolnshire* (Macmillan, 1926)

Rudkin, E. H., *Lincolnshire Folklore* (Beltons, Gainsborough, 1936)

Satchell, T., *For Better or Worse* (Craftsman Press, 2003)

Simpson, J. & Roud, S., *A Dictionary of English Folklore* (Oxford University Press, 2001)

Trubshaw, B., *Explore Folklore* (Explore Books, 2002)

Underwood, P., *No Common Task* (Harrap, 1983)

Westwood, J. & Simpson, J., *The Lore of the Land* (Penguin, 2005)

Whittington-Egan, R., *Liverpool Colonnade* (Philip Son & Nephew, 1955)

⚜ ARTICLES ⚜

Everson, P. & Stocker, D., 'Sex, Self-Censorship and the Anglo-Saxonist',
   Lincolnshire Past and Present, No. 42, Winter 2000/2001, p. 306
Healey, H., 'A Willoughby Connection in Oxfordshire', *Lincolnshire Past
   and Present*, No. 42, Winter 2000/2001, p. 11
Simons, P., 'Weather Eye', *The Times*, 7 October, 2010
Swaby, J.E., 'The Louth Imps', *Lincolnshire Past and Present*, No. 42, Winter
   2000, pp. 16–17

⚜ NEWSPAPERS AND PERIODICALS ⚜

Hobart Mercury
Lincolnshire History and Archaeology
Lincolnshire Life
Lincolnshire Magazine
Lincolnshire Past and Present
The Poacher
The Times Digital Archive

⚜ WEBSITES ⚜

http://lincolnshiregothic.blogspot.com/
http://www.lincslouthmclassic.co.uk/sir_hickman_bacon
http://www.sheelanagig.org/main.htm
http://www.thebookofdays.com/months/march/20.html

INDEX

Other titles published by The History Press

Hanged at Lincoln
STEPHEN WADE

This intriguing book gathers together the stories of 120 criminals hanged at both Lincoln Castle Prison and HMP Lincoln on Greetwell Road between 1203 and 1961. Fully illustrated with photographs, drawings, news cuttings and documents, *Hanged at Lincoln* will appeal to everyone interested in the shadier side of Lincoln's history.

978 0 7509 5110 4

Lincolnshire Murders
STEPHEN WADE

This fascinating exploration of Lincolnshire's criminal history will intrigue and horrify. in equal measure. It contains both famous cases and little-known mysteries, including three unsolved homicides and a murder trial in which the victim's dog appeared as a key witness in court.

978 0 7509 4321 5

Murder & Crime in Lincoln
DOUGLAS WYNN

John Haig, the acid-bath murderer, was born in nearby Stamford, and was imprisoned in Lincoln (where he experimented on small animals to perfect his acid-bath techniques). In this book, combining meticulous research with evocative photography, the author provides a feast of crime to haunt the imagination of any reader.

978 0 7524 5921 9

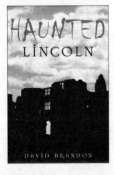

Haunted Lincoln
DAVID BRANDON

The city of Lincoln groans under the weight of thousands of years of history. Not surprisingly, this ancient city is rife with tales of spirits. This in-depth introduction, with a glossary of spooky terms, is included to guide the reader on their spine-tingling journey around the city.

978 0 7524 4891 6

Visit our website and discover thousands of other History Press books.

www.thehistorypress.co.uk